moin

"Remember, remember always, that all of us, you and I especially, are descended from immigrants and revolutionaries."

–Franklin Delano Roosevelt

Gitta

Johanna, Julia, Maja, Alexander, and Leonard

ISBN 978-0-9912758-3-0

Second Edition June 2017

© Copyright 2017 by Stoltenberg Institute for German-American Forty-Eighter Studies

103 N. Orchard St.; Northfield, MN; 55057; USA

yogireppmann@gmail.com — www.Moin-Moin.us

Benjamin Parsell, Minnesota, Webmaster, bsparsell@gmail.com

Dietrich Eicke, Bad Oldesloe, www.eickeweb.de, designed moin Logo.

Georg Wawerla, Kiel, www.studio38-kiel.de, designed 1848er Logo.

Crossing the Ocean

Part One

Chapters

Table of Contents

Preface

The American Dream

"The promise and security of living as a free individual in a community founded on the pursuit of happiness and individual freedoms."

BY ERHARD "BOEDDEE" BÖTTCHER, A FREQUENT TRAVELER TO THE UNITED STATES

Each and every citizen of the United States, each and every immigrant, knows and lives with the promise of the American Dream, as expressed by three extraordinary monuments of literature.

The Declaration of Independence from the year 1776 states: "We hold these truths to be self-evident, that all men are created equal, that they are endowed by their Creator with certain unalienable rights, that among these are life, liberty, and the pursuit of happiness."

"The New Colossus," a poem written in 1883 by the American poet Emma Lazarus, is engraved on the pedestal of the Statue of Liberty in New York harbor. The final and most important lines say: "Give me your tired, your poor, your huddled masses yearning to breathe free, the wretched refuse of your teeming shore. Send these, the homeless, tempest-tossed to me: I lift my lamp beside the golden door."

More recently, the historic speech by Martin Luther King on August 28, 1963, expresses the obligation that the American Dream be fulfilled for everyone in the United States, regardless of race: "I have a dream that my four little children will one day live in a nation where they will not be judged by the color of their skin, but by the content of their character."

We will explore the status of this great American Dream in the pages that follow.

WHERE GERMAN ROOTS RUN DEEP

Germans first came to
America in large
numbers in the 1720s,
when many settled in
Pennsylvania. A second
and much larger wave
began in the 1830s and
lasted until 1930, with
most going to the
Midwest and the upper
Plains states. In 1790,
only 7 percent of the
American population
was of German descent.
Today, people who list
German ancestry first
on the census form
make up 23 percent of
the population.

Share of Americans who list German
ancestry first on the census form,
by county

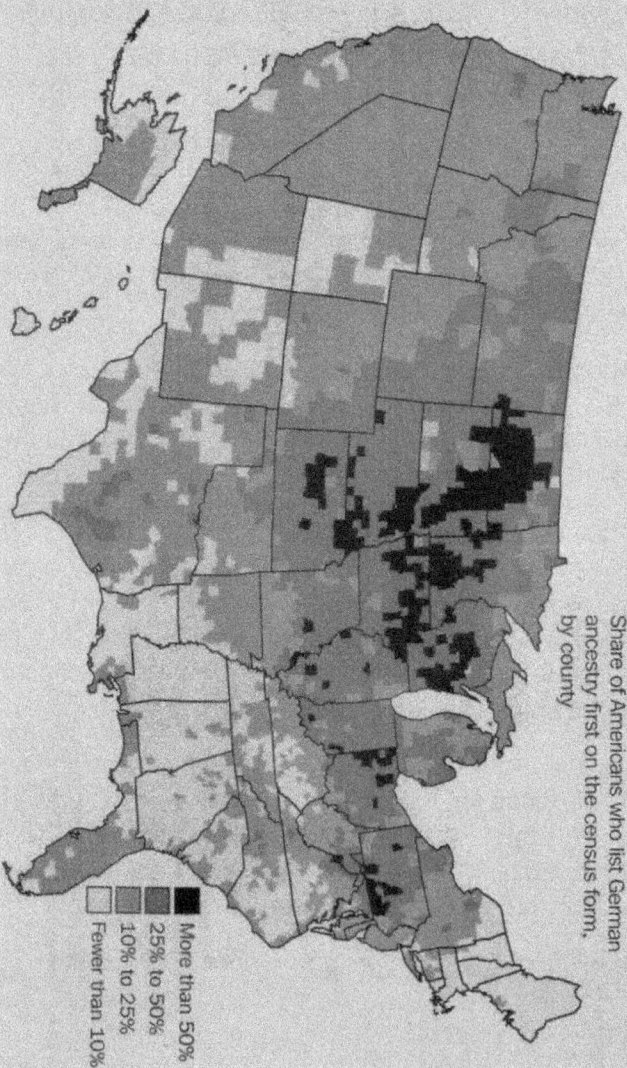

Legend:
- More than 50%
- 25% to 50%
- 10% to 25%
- Fewer than 10%

Foreword

Freedom & Self-determination

BASED ON A NEWSPAPER REPORT FOR THE

FLENSBURG JOURNAL BY DIETER E. WILHELMY

A merica? What does that mean? Washington and Trump? The wealthy stockbrokers on Wall Street, or the homeless people who sleep on pieces of cardboard in storefronts? Actors who become politicians, or politicians who act like actors? The megacities of the east and west coasts, or the endless expanses of the Midwest?

All of the above, and much more. And German impressions of the United States are equally varied. Many see only what they regard as the negative aspects of American culture, others take a positive view. These perspectives have changed to some degree over the years. The well-known cliché of "the land of opportunity" prevailed in the nineteenth century, while in the twentieth Germans came to admire Americans' jazzy (and later pop) music, their casual demeanor, and—much later—their digital revolution.

Dr. Joachim "Yogi" Reppmann, a historian who was born in Flensburg, a German city in the state of Schleswig-Holstein that borders on Denmark, is privileged to have homes in both the "old" and the "new" world. For over twenty-five years Yogi and his wife Gitta have spent six months of the year in his hometown in northern Germany, and the other in Northfield, Minnesota, in the Midwest of the United States. It was to this "heartland" that thousands emigrated from Germany a century-and-a-half ago, not to escape from poverty, as is sometimes assumed, but to seek freedom from repression following the failed democratic revolution of 1848. They had only one goal in mind: freedom and self-determination. These basic principles, including responsibility for oneself and for the community, have always characterized the American way of thinking.

The history of the Forty-Eighters' emigration has become the Flensburg historian's greatest research interest. It was not only the parliamentarians who met in Frankfurt's St. Paul's Church, but also the democrats Theodore and Justus Olshausen from Schleswig-Holstein, who made contributions to the idea of creating a German state based on a liberal constitution. The failure of this early republican attempt and the subsequent emigration of many influential "48er" intellectuals to the United States had a lasting effect on the development of American history.

A presentation of Yogi's experiences in the United States over the years will help provide us, as readers, with access to the American "soul." (Cf. interview p. 47)

Erinnerung an zwei „48er"

Christian-Albrechts-Universität ehrt die Brüder Theodor und Justus Olshausen mit einer eigenen

Kiel – Obwohl die Olshausenstraße gewissermaßen die Central Avenue der Universität darstellt, lässt sich heute nicht mehr rekonstruieren, ob ihr Name auf Theodor oder seinen Bruder Justus Olshausen Bezug nimmt. Als Vorkämpfer der Demokratie während der 1848er Revolution hätten beide es verdient – weshalb ihnen die Alma Mater nun eine eigene Gedenkstele widmet.

Von Oliver Stenzel

Der eine war ein bedeutender Gelehrter, der andere ein umtriebiger Journalist und Verleger. Gemeinsam war Justus und Theodor Olshausen ihr engagiertes Eintreten für die Demokratie in der Mitte des 19. Jahrhunderts. Während der Kieler Orientalistik-Pro-

Kieler Nachrichten (Kiel Daily Newspaper) June 6 , 2009, reporting about a new Theodore and Justus Olshausen 1848er memorial installation, located on Olshausenstrasse, the main street that runs through the Kiel university campus in the State of Schleswig-Holstein. Professor Fouquet, University President, Yogi Reppmann, event manager, and Cathy Kietzer, Kiel City President.

Chapter 1

The Ideal of America

Never in my wildest dreams did I ever think that my life would develop as it has. Even when I was a child America was the land of my longings. The person responsible for this wanderlust was Karl May, one of the most successful, most productive writers of Western stories in the world—and one who, in America of all places, is virtually unknown.

Although narrow-chested and shy, I never avoided a fight when I was a boy. I often saw myself as Old Shatterhand, who, strong as a bear, rode with the Apache chieftain Winnetou across the wide prairie on his horse Hatatit-la. In my fantasy, the sofa in my parents' apartment became a buffalo I had bagged and behind which I looked for cover in a battle with hostile Indians.

As a boy I spent my summers with my grandparents in Jena in what was then communist East Germany. There I could watch television to my heart's content. On the "Black Channel," a politically-oriented station of the GDR, the world was seen exclusively through the deep-red lens of "true socialism." In their view, our peace-loving friends were in charge in the Soviet Union, whereas the United States was ruled by blood-thirsty warmongers.

It's surprising to see what accumulated in the mind of a boy like me at that time. In 1968, for example, airplane hijackings from America to Cuba were commonplace. In East Germany, news like this was exploited to the hilt. The hijackings were seen as unequivocal proof of the suppression of Americans, who supposedly could escape this only by fleeing to Fidel Castro's Communist Cuba. In reality the hijackers were either left-wing radicals or small-time criminals who hoped to extort ransom money from the U. S. government or the airline. For communist East Germany, however, these people were without exception victims of political persecution.

Those were stormy times. Anti-war demonstrations in the United States, student unrest in Paris followed by a general strike, riots in Switzerland, peace marches in Germany that sometimes resulted in bloodied heads.

1961, shortly before the Wall was built: With "Grandma Jena" on the way to her allotment garden in East Germany. The Iron Curtain /the Wall (in actuality two walls) was built during the Cold War and separated East and West Germany, East and West Berlin, NATO and the Warsaw Pact, western "world capitalism" from eastern European communism.

"Ami Go Home!"

Young people throughout the world were in an uproar. There were protests. Everywhere and against everything. In my north German hometown of Flensburg, too, of course. Especially at my school, known simply as the "Old High." Young people protested against the Vietnam War or against raising the prices of bus and streetcar tickets or against antiquated educational practices or against the Nazi past of the older generation. I got involved in everything. Little Yogi and his friends always sat in the very front row on the street. But when the "bulls," as we disrespectfully called policemen, arrived with their nightsticks, we disappeared on the spot and ran home to hide under our mothers' skirts.

And so the years between 1968 and 1971 went by. The true activists, who mostly chanted "Ho Ho Ho-Chi-Minh" or "Ami go home" in the streets of West Berlin, were staunch opponents of so-called U. S. imperialism. The odd thing about the whole business was that they borrowed the protest terms, such as "sit-in" or "teach-in," from American English. Beyond that, their clothes and hairdos were American in style, and they listened to British and American music. They fought against pluralism as an ideology that disguised capitalist class rule while at the same time contributing to the Federal Republic's becoming more pluralistic after 1968 than ever before.

In many cases, the individual movements differed significantly from each other. When the Afro-American track-and-field medalists Tommie Smith and John Carlos raised their black-gloved fists at the 1968 summer Olympic Games in Mexico City following the murder of Martin Luther King, they were fighting for Black Power and the equal treatment of minorities. For its part, the flower-power and hippie movement was committed to sexual freedom. Its mottoes went something like this: "Don't sleep twice with a girl or a gent, 'cause that's what they do in the Establishment."

If for once I wasn't protesting against something, or signing leaflets (unread) on the school grounds, I would be defending my positive image of America vehemently. My classmates couldn't relate to this at all and thought I was an absolute idiot. That didn't bother me, though. To this very day I'm enormously grateful to the Americans who fought against hunger in Europe after the Second World War and secured the freedom of West Berlin in 1948/49 through the Berlin Airlift.

Hitchhiking in North America

My "Karl May" dream became reality several years later, when I completed my secondary schooling in 1976 and, shouldering my backpack, took a flight to New York with Thies Matzen, a pal from dancing class. I had never met an American before, aside from one exchange student named Roger Smith. And with only a slip of paper with the boy's address and the bold plan of hitchhiking through as many U. S. states and Canadian provinces as possible, we two Flensburgers landed in the metropolis.

In genuine American fashion, we were welcomed with open arms by Roger's parents and became their week-long guests. Then began the trip we had dreamt of, through southern Canada, the northwest of the United States, and from there to San Francisco and the warm South of New Orleans and Florida. We hitched rides, slept in the open, spent one night in a motel in Las Vegas and were welcomed wholeheartedly by total strangers and treated fantastically well. I was especially impressed by the positive attitude toward life of most Americans, their curiosity, their civility and willingness to help. It was this first trip to the United States that set the course for my entire future life.

Flensburg, Minnesota - 284 inhabitants.

Subsequent American Adventures

My Lübeck university friend Dietrich (Dee) Eicke and I were clearly naïve as we set out in 1978 on a three-month research trip to the United States with the financial help of Schleswig-Holstein Prime Minister Gerhard Stoltenberg. Bearded and long-haired at the time, we had a conference with one of the minister's assistants and, to the astonishment of everyone including ourselves, were granted financial aid for our project. Our plan was to explore the roots of Schleswig-Holstein place names, but during our trip we discovered far more than simply American towns called Schleswig, Holstein, Husum, Lubec, and Flensburg—we discovered a world that was new to us.

Top: Schleswig, Western Iowa, was founded in 1899.
Bottom: The City of Holstein, Iowa - see biography about Virginia Degen, p. 54.

"Uncultured America"

Those who have done research in creaky old European libraries with dusty bookshelves, where simply taking out a book causes a stomach ache, can barely contain their amazement when they visit American museums and libraries. Apart from the wealth of materials available, the buildings themselves look more like splendid palaces. By comparison, the archives in Schleswig or Copenhagen are unprepossessing cottages. This was the impression my friend Dee Eicke and I had during our second trip to the United States in 1982, which marked the beginning of our serious work of research. For four long months we spent as much as ten hours a day rummaging through archives, libraries, and museums, or interviewing residents of communities with names that had their origins in Schleswig-Holstein and who were experts on the subject of the history of their city.

Our first visit was to the Historical Society in New York, a gigantic building on the corner of Central Park West and 77th Street. Since its founding in 1804, researchers have been studying the history of the city of New York, the state of New York, and the United States in general. The building houses an extensive library of manuscripts, newspapers, and other documents covering a span of four centuries.

In this archive we found among other things the first book by Rudolf Puchner, who settled in the very young community of New Holstein, Wisconsin in 1849. As the owner of a general store he came into contact with members of every social stratum and recorded significant impressions and experiences at the time. When we came upon his book it seemed to us that we had unearthed an immense treasure, if only one made of paper. As for Dee and myself, we were as poor as church mice. To save on hotel costs, we had built up a network of friends and acquaintances who could put us up for a time. In New York, that person was Thaddäus Schnugg, a Flensburger who lived with the Broadway dancer and choreographer George Faison. Along with our daily work at the Historical Society, we got to know through him a completely new and unknown world of dancers and musicians, including the renowned band "Earth, Wind, and Fire."

For our continuing journey, Faison recommended us to friends in his hometown of Washington. There we stayed with a married couple in the African-American district. On the porches in front of the little houses sat jobless men with a can of beer in their hand. They gave us friendly greetings as we walked by and asked "How are you?" or "Where are you from?" We appeared to be the only white people in this ghetto, where many of the houses were more like nailed-together dog houses. The gangs ruled here; people dealt drugs and we heard gunshots on occasion. Washington was the murder capital of the United States. But we weren't afraid, for whatever reason. Maybe because there were two of us, or maybe because we were young and carefree.

Today everything is new here. The houses, the stores, the clubs. BMWs drive around in the old neighborhoods, along with brand-new Fords blasting hip-hop music.

Washington – "Chocolate City"

The White House, only a few minutes away by car, is in a different world. Down in the historic center stand the majestic buildings, monuments to American history: the President's home, the Capitol, the Lincoln Memorial, to name only a few. Almost everyone is familiar with this white marble face of Washington. Even so, D. C. is a traditional "chocolate city." Far more than half of its residents are black. For almost a hundred years, America's minority has been the majority here.

Our goal every day was Capitol Hill, where the three buildings of the Library of Congress stand, each in a different architectural style. The oldest is the Thomas Jefferson Building, inaugurated in 1897 and impressive in its Italian Renaissance style, with its magnificent marble entrance hall. The architecture of the John Adams Building, in use since 1938, is characterized by Art Nouveau elements, while the sober, six-story James Mason Memorial Building had been dedicated in 1980, only two years before our trip to America. More than four thousand co-workers are employed in this gigantic complex.

The Gutenberg Bible

The Library of Congress is the second-largest in the world, after the British Library in London. Its holdings include 151,785,778 books and other printed matter in 470 languages; of these, fifty million are manuscripts, twelve million are photographs, and almost five million are maps and charts. An extremely rare item, one of forty-nine still in existence, is the Gutenberg Bible housed on the basement level.

Our knowledge about the immigration of Schleswig-Holsteiners and the 1848ers in particular grew day by day. The latter were proponents of a republican form of government and came to establish a new homeland in America following the failed revolutionary movement in Europe. Leading Schleswig-Holsteiners in the circle of Theodore Olshausen (1802-1869) and Hans Reimer Claussen (1804-1894) settled in Davenport, Iowa on the Mississippi, two hours west of Chicago by car today.

A Success Story

In the Library of Congress we also found documents about Ludwig Nissen from the town of Husum, who left his parental house in 1872 and became a diamond merchant in New York. His was a typical "made in America" career: he began as a bootblack, washed dishes, worked as a waiter and cashier, and later became a butcher and innkeeper. He eventually opened a jewelry store on Fifth Avenue, New York's most elegant street, with a fellow German named Fred Schilling. Nissen died childless in Brooklyn in 1924, but his connection to his homeland was never broken, and he named the town of Husum as heir to his great fortune. Today the North Sea Museum of Husum, the City Library, and the Café Brütt are housed in the Ludwig Nissen House. The urn containing his ashes is kept under the cupola of the building's rotunda.

The United States is very young in comparison with the countries of Europe. In spite of this, it has an exemplary system of archives that contain even today many undiscovered treasures. My traveling companion and I had our next archival experience in Madison, the capital of Wisconsin. The State Historical Society there is a combination of archive and library, and possesses the largest collection of German-American books in the United States. Here we investigated the origins and development of the small town of New Holstein, Wisconsin, a community that was founded on democratic principles in 1848 by Schleswig-Holsteiners.

Ludwig Nissen, Husum & New York.

Our professor of American Studies at the University of Kiel, Paul G. Buchloh, encountered massive opposition when he advanced the thesis during a lecture in Husum that the New York diamond merchant Ludwig Nissen from Husum might have become fabulously wealthy through the illegal slave trade. We tried unsuccessfully in New York and Washington, D.C. to find out whether there still were frozen accounts in Nissen's name following America's entry into World War I.

Chapter 2

New Holstein

The Awakening to Freedom

Ich kann den Blick nicht von euch wenden,
Ich muss euch anschaun immerdar:
Wie reicht ihr mit geschäftgen Händen
Dem Schiffer eure Habe dar!

I cannot look away from you,
I stare and stare, and cannot cease;
As all your goods pass to the crew
I stare and stare and have no peace.

-FERDINAND FREILIGRATH, 1832

Ferdinand Freiligrath (1810-1876), a freedom fighter and poet of the German revolution of 1848, was an early eyewitness to the beginning of the mass emigration of Germans to North America. In the above excerpt from his poem "Der Auswanderer," Freiligrath expresses the emigrants' mixed feelings: disappointment and yearning, self-confidence and firmness of purpose, a longing for faraway places and faith in the future. Beyond the broad Atlantic, they knew, lay the land of hope.

The year 1848 was a turning point in the history of democratic revolutions in Europe, especially in Schleswig-Holstein. The important heritage left by the so-called "Forty-Eighters" is little known to most people, both in Germany and the United States. With its political and moral ideals, under the motto "freedom, education, and prosperity for all," it could be a model in today's world as well for our involvement in state and society. Following their arrival in the United States, the Forty-Eighters realized their life's dream and bequeathed to their descendants values that had a lasting effect on American society.

The Call of Wisconsin's Wilderness: New Holstein, 1848

As the wagons of the seventy immigrants rumbled across the wooden planks that formed a road through the wilderness, many a deep sigh could no doubt be heard. So this was to be their new homeland. Banks of fog drifted over the countless swamps, and from the almost impenetrable forests rifle shots and the cries of huntsmen resounded. This was home to Indians, trappers, and fur hunters.

The primeval region that would later be called New Holstein was located in Wisconsin, between Lake Michigan to the east and Lake Winnebago to the west. It was to be made arable in accordance with the notions of a man named Wilhelm Ostenfeld. After breaking off his study of law in Kiel in 1843, he had sought his fortune in far-off America and settled in Calumetville on Lake Winnebago. In 1847 he traveled by ship to Hamburg with his American friend Charles White. The sole purpose of their trip was to recruit people who were willing to emigrate. They were successful in the far northern cities of Kiel, Itzehoe, Heide, Flensburg, among others.

Ostenfeld and White had tossed together a motley crew of people who dared to make the leap into an uncertain future. None of them knew any of the others. At the end of March they met in Hamburg and boarded the emigrant ship "Brarens." It left Hamburg on April 2, 1848 and arrived in New York on May 12. The winds were favorable and the forty-day crossing bearable, even though offerings were made to Neptune every now and then. The violent spring storms that churn up the North Sea and the Atlantic every year had abated. Just one year later another Atlantic crossing of the "Brarens" ended in catastrophe, as the ship ran aground at Ramsgate in England near the end of its trip from New York.

The Revolution in Kiel

It was not utter want or starvation that these people were fleeing, but a dependent, subjugated existence and a seeming lack of prospects for the future. In Schleswig-Holstein the political situation had come to a head on March 24, 1848 with the founding of a German provisional government in Kiel and the overpowering of the Danish fortress of Rendsburg. This was of course a daily topic of conversation among the group of Forty-Eighter emigrants. They heard nothing, however, of the defeat on April 9, 1848 of the Schleswig-Holstein freedom fighters by the Danish government troops at Bau, before the gates of Flensburg, since the "Brarens" was already well on its way across the ocean at that time.

1978: Dee Eicke and Yogi Reppmann in the 1848er Museum in New Holstein, WI. They are studying portraits of a married couple named Schildhauer, who came from Schleswig-Holstein to America via Brazil, and whose son Edward Schildhauer developed the lock technology used in the Panama Canal.

Leatherstocking as a Model

The Schleswig-Holsteiners who wanted to start a new, free life in America associated their future homeland with romantic notions. This was the case with the physician Dr. Karl Bock, who had all his knowledge from books. His preferred reading apparently was the bestseller of the time, *Leatherstocking*, by James Fenimore Cooper. While taking a walk with his wife, he went into raptures: "the Indians in Cooper's *Leatherstocking*, my source for knowledge of this nation, are the kindliest people with a praiseworthy manner of living. The freest people on earth . . . obliged only to hunt and fish, and with the prospect of entering an especially beautiful heaven some day."

Though the immigrants' expectations were not always realistic, their desire for freedom eclipsed everything. The prospect of creating a new settlement from the ground up with their compatriots made any fears of uncertainty dwindle. They were only too happy to turn their backs on the authoritarian system back home in order to lead a life of freedom.

The North Germans were spared any bitter disappointments during their trip. Wilhelm Ostenfeld and Charles White were prudent leaders, and the new arrivals in New York did not become victims of the "runners" who were hanging about. These swindlers were often former fellow countrymen who were easily able to gain the confidence of the unsuspecting and take advantage of them mercilessly by arranging for food or living quarters at outrageously high prices.

Few of the various passengers—eight single travelers, two married couples, and fifty-eight family members—had financial worries. Twelve of them were able to afford cabin rooms on the ship, and over the thousand-mile trip from New York to Calumetville, much of this by railroad, numerous suitcases and boxes containing valuable items were transported. One chronicle stated that many people carried gold pieces. They were accustomed to a standard of living that could hardly be matched in the backwoods or on the prairies. So what could they have been looking for that their homeland didn't offer them? It had to be political freedom.

The Founding of a Town

The settlement area of Calumet County covered 778 square kilometers (327 square miles). In this area, roughly as large as a German city, 850 people lived scattered in 1848. Later, in New Holstein—listed in the land register as Town 17, Range 20—there were precisely 22 people, who had arrived six years earlier from South Germany.

Drawing in a letter from New Holstein, Wisconsin dated June 5, 1850, from Andreas F. Hanssen, 1811-1860, a native of Schenefeld (north of Hamburg) and the editor of the 'Altona Mercury,' to his famous brother, the agricultural historian Prof. Georg Hanssen: "... If for nothing more, I could envy you your six children, as I have already said. In several days my house will be finished . . ., then I will seriously start looking for a wife . . . Here in America, such things go quickly." (Georg considered emigrating to New Holstein for several years. In the Special Collection of the State Historical Society of Wisconsin in Madison we found a series of letters from Andreas to Georg Hanssen in Göttingen, and also long letters from Dorpat, Riga, Lisbon, and New Holstein.)

On the very same day that Wisconsin became the thirtieth state of the United States, May 29, 1848, the future founders reached their longed-for goal. Agreements for the purchase of land were negotiated on the spot, and workers from Calumetville were given jobs building houses.

Bit by bit, nature was overcome. Trees were felled, wells dug, fields tilled. The style of the buildings that grew up out of the soil were nothing like those in the old country. No one tried to preserve typically north German structures in this new world. People did without thatched roofs as well as red tiles, which would in any case have been difficult to come by. They even said farewell to the usual way of living they had once known. The family, the cattle, and the harvested crops no longer were found under the same roof. In short, the new arrivals accustomed themselves to their new environment. As one New Holsteiner described his neighbor's house: "The owner, Herr Arens from Dithmarschen, stepped toward us from under an overhang that was supported by graceful columns."

The acquired properties were almost without exception between 80 and 160 acres, occasionally even as much as 200 acres. By comparison, on farms in the Federal Republic of today an average of 139 acres are cultivated.

The professions of the first settlers can be found in the ship register of the "Brarens." Only four men are listed as manual workers, and many of the passengers had some degree of higher education. An entry next to the name Karl Grüning even states "master of Latin and English language." For such immigrants, their American counterparts had the brief and fitting term "Latin farmers"—meaning that they had greater knowledge of Horace and Ovid than of rock-hard field work.

A "new" Holstein in America

Wilhelm Ostenfeld had the idea of giving Town 17 the name New Holstein while he was still on board the "Brarens." His reason was "not only to remind ourselves of the land of our heritage, but also to serve as a signpost which future immigrants from the duchies will gladly decide to use as a guide."

Historians have argued vehemently as to why the town was named *New* Holstein and what political motivation there could have been for this. Regardless of whether the first settlers hoped to found a "new Germany" or not, they may well have been inspired by the idea of constructing a community based on republican principles in the middle of a primeval forest.

Back home in Germany, word of the founding of New Holstein spread rapidly. In 1848 more Germans continued to arrive. By 1855 the stream of immigrants had stopped. The Schleswig-Holsteiners represented the greatest share of the population, amounting to 65 percent in 1860 as opposed to the almost 30 percent of other Germans. Inhabitants without German roots were in the minority, only 5.5 percent. Many farmers settled in the neighboring township of Schleswig, which was also established at that time. Back then there still was plenty of free land.

German Societies

An intermixing of the various parts of the population did not take place. People kept to themselves—the Germans here, the others elsewhere. And where there are Germans, there are clubs. In 1849 a choral society had already been founded, one in which the singing was even accompanied by piano. The instrument belonged to a music lover from Dithmarschen who had brought it with him across the ocean. An oratorical society was also established in this year, consisting of twenty men who met every two weeks to conduct debates in the form of a sporting competition. The Dramatic Society followed in 1854, a Lutheran Society in 1857, and finally, in 1867, a gymnastics club (Turnverein). The Dramatic Society enjoyed putting on occasional stage productions. Against the background of the European upheavals the favorite author was Friedrich Schiller, the proponent of freedom ("Man is created free, is free, even if born in chains"). His play *Love and Intrigue* was a gigantic success.

German Gemütlichkeit was also alive and well in these societies. Every now and then there were huge celebrations, at which one or the other immigrant could wash away his homesickness with a swallow or two of beer. The societies offered their members at least a minimum dose of homeland, a place where they could speak German and maintain the old traditions.

Several hundred miles away, in the little town of Holstein (without the modifier "New") in the state of Iowa, a ring tournament and bird-shooting contest (Voogelscheeten) was put on every year by the local gymnastics club. Interestingly, no similar activities are known to have taken place in

New Holstein, apart from a large-scale festival to which people were invited by the gymnastics club in 1875. This fair was more like the South German Oktoberfest, however, which is surprising for a locale in which the majority of the inhabitants were native Schleswig-Holsteiners and their children.

The gymnastics clubs were of great significance in the German towns. Apart from New Holstein, where people were mostly content with the simplicity of their lives, these clubs were centers where the liberal ideas of the revolution of 1848 were fiercely defended. The first German gymnastics club on American soil was founded in Cincinnati in 1848. The club's declared goal, along with gymnastic exercise as a counter to spiritual and material pressures, was the insistence on genuine freedom, prosperity, and education for all classes of society.

This in turn created suspicion in many of the non-German Americans. They observed with mistrust the aspirations of the Germans, for whom aspects of American reality had been disappointing. During the European revolutionary movements of 1848 they had put their lives on the line for freedom, and what did they find in America? Slavery! They became declared opponents of slaveholding.

The Civil War

When the Civil War broke out in 1861, German immigrants took up arms almost without exception and with great conviction. They fought on the side of Abraham Lincoln and in doing so made their declaration both for their new homeland and for freedom. Several exclusively German regiments were formed, among them the 9th Wisconsin Infantry.

After the victory of the northern states over the South, the gymnastics clubs joined together to form the North American Gymnastics Alliance. Their goals had changed with the abolishment of slavery. The radical political character of the clubs was replaced with physical training, the nurturing of good fellowship, and commitment to social matters.

Until the construction of a gymnasium in the year 1872, New Holstein Turners (from turnen = to do gymnastics) met in the evening hours and carried out their exercise routines in a hotel run by a Herr Luethge. Before heading for home, whether on foot, by wagon, or on horseback, they sat for a while in the hotel guest room drinking a glass of beer and enjoying each other's company. They were proud of their exercises on the horizontal and parallel bars, and with justification. In fact, the *Milwaukee Sentinel*, an American daily newspaper, praised the group in 1887 in its best "Denglish": "The New Holstein Riesenriege (squad of giants) was the center of attraction at the state Turnfest."

Newspapers in German

German-language newspapers in the United States look back on a long tradition. On July 5, 1776 the *Pennsylvanischer Staatsbote* (Pennsylvanian State Messenger) reported on the decision of the Continental Congress to accept the Americans' declaration of independence. In doing this, it became the first newspaper to publish this historic decision and to print the text in German translation. By the end of the nineteenth century there were hundreds of German-language newspapers, which had great influence on the immigrants as they slowly grew into their new environment. For the German 1848er revolutionary and subsequent American politician Carl Schurz (1829-1906), the task of these papers was to explain the nature of America to those countrymen who knew no English and in effect to become a connecting link between the old and new homelands.

In the state of Iowa, German-language newspapers were available in several communities in the nineteenth century. The earliest of these was *Der Demokrat*, published in Davenport starting in 1851. Among its first editors were the Schleswig-Holstein freedom fighters Theodore Gülich and Theodore Olshausen; criticism of Prussian government policies resulted in the banning of this American publication in Prussia. As is evident in its name, *Der Demokrat* was a strong supporter of social reforms and was equally opposed to slavery. Like many other German-language newspapers, it endured well into the twentieth century but eventually ceased publishing due to anti-German sentiment during the First World War.

Theodore Olshausen ►

◄ *Theodore Gülich*

A woodcut showing the second motto and logo of Der Demokrat.

From August P. Richter, Geschichte der Stadt Davenport und des County Scott, (Davenport, IA: originally printed by the Fred Klein Co., 1917), 471.

On November 15, 1851, the first issue of the Davenport German language newspaper *Der Demokrat* appeared. The motto Suum cuique, a Latin phrase popularized by Cicero that originated from the old Greek principle of justice, "to each his own," accompanied the newspaper's title, which was produced in large, ornate Latin characters. Soon thereafter, the caption was typeset in German (Jedem das Seine!) and enveloped by a satirical panorama. Dr. August Paul Richter described this symbolic representation as follows:

"In a background of prison castles, turrets, keeps and gallows, one sees a society of princely personages, Jesuits and other reactionaries, with Lola Montez dancing before them. Farther to the front strides the 'popular purveyor of God's grace' in festive parade, Friedrich Wilhelm IV (Champagne Fritz), followed by Tsar Nicholas, the youthful Franz Joseph, the Pope and Louis Napoleon. Democrats in dense masses, who apparently do not wish to be thus graced, press to the harbor, which is covered by steamers and sailboats, as is the bay. In the New World the men for freedom are greeted with a roaring welcome, even by priests and bible society supporters, past whom they hurry to the trains to take them to the west."

The *Davenporter Turngemeinde,* founded 1852, was the city's most recognized German organization. The Turners endeavored to improve mankind physically, ethically, intellectually, and culturally. Their goal was a more "refined humanity," and their leaders regarded the Turnverein as a vital educational force for cultural progress, freedom, and good citizenship. Through lectures and public discussion, members of the Turnverein were at the forefront in promoting suffrage for women. German feminist and newspaper editor Mathilde Franziska Anneke "justifies the claim that they were among the founders of the women's liberation movement."

Davenport has also spawned several well-known German-American politicians. Included in this number are Forty-Eighter Nicholas Johann Rusch, Iowa's second lieutenant governor; Forty-Eighter Hans Reimer Claussen, a state senator; Forty-Eighter Ernst Carl Olrog Claussen, a seven-term mayor of Davenport; Forty-Eighter Matthias Jensen Rohlfs, a four-term state representative and city treasurer for fourteen years; and Henry Vollmer, Davenport's "boy mayor," who assumed that office when only twenty-six years of age and who went on to represent Iowa in the U. S. House of Representatives.

One can scarcely discuss the economic history of Davenport and Scott County without paying homage to the German immigrant. So thoroughly did he dominate farming in and around Davenport. But German-Americans' inroad into Davenport's economic life was certainly not limited to agriculture, as they and their descendants quickly played key roles in wholesale and retail, manufacturing, banking, publishing, and in various service industries. See: Scott C. Christiansen, *The Argument for digitizing Davenport's preeminent German language newspaper, 'Der Demokrat', 96-121,* in: Yearbook 2016, The Stoltenberg Institute for German-American Forty-Eighter Studies, Northfield, MN / Flensburg, 2016. (www.LuLu.com)

By contrast, the town of New Holstein in Wisconsin never did have its own German-language paper. The first residents were able to read about world events in only two newspapers, the English *Milwaukee Sentinel* and the German *Milwaukee Herold*. This second paper was probably the more widely-read of the two in the beginning. In 1889 the weekly German paper *Nachrichten aus Schleswig-Holstein* appeared in Oak Park, a suburb of Chicago. Its publishers were, however, first and foremost interested in fostering the German language and reported virtually nothing about American matters. Its readership in nearby New Holstein was minuscule, and the *Kiel National-Zeitung*, founded in a neighboring town in 1893. also found little response there. Most of New Holstein's residents had become Americans in body and soul by then; as a sole source of information, German-language newspapers had outlived their usefulness for them.

Difficulties with the Mail

On April 2, 1849 a significant day dawned for New Holstein: the little settlement was granted independent status and thereby all the rights and duties of self-government. Until this point it had been administered by the neighboring Brothertown. Eight years later streets and plots of land were surveyed and the "Village of Altona" was entered in the land register of Chilton, the county seat. Later on it was named "Village of New Holstein" out of practical reasons, since there was a town of Altoona (with a double "o") farther to the west of Wisconsin, and this led to serious mix-ups with mail deliveries.

The typical American placemats in the Altona Supper Club in New Holstein inform each guest about the founding of the city by the 1848er democratic republicans from Schleswig-Holstein. — In 1982 we bought an 8-cylinder Chevy for $300 in New York City; the woman selling it had lovingly given her "dream car" the name Black Beauty.

Life in New Holstein was truly peaceful. In 1861 a road was finally constructed that connected the town with Lake Michigan. It was originally made out of wooden planks and was the major connection to the world beyond. The situation was further improved with the extension of the railroad to New Holstein at a cost of $30,000; train travel to Madison and Milwaukee, sixty miles away, was now possible.

A Swabian with a "Yankee Eye"

Two Swabians, H. Bruckmann and Rudolf Puchner, gave the town an important boost in 1849 by opening a general store. Puchner turned out to be a clever fellow. He had lived in New York for six months and during that short stay had acquired "a real Yankee eye," as he himself said.

Everything was available in the store. Clothing for the whole family, tools for the house and garden, firearms and ammunition, and all sorts of odds and ends. There was hardly a thing that he and his associate did not have in stock. Business was good, and money jingled in the cash register. Puchner was not only a good businessman, but also a lover of beauty whose passion was writing. His romantic poems were published in a little book called *Klänge aus dem Westen* (Sounds of the West). He also spent many an evening recording items of local interest by petroleum lamp and eventually developed into an important chronicler. (Puchner's book is mentioned on page 20 of our text.)

Among other things he recorded the story of Nikolaus Vollstedt, a tall and powerful fellow who would tackle any job with great energy. By 1854 he had become fed up with his life in Germany. Leaving the cathedral city of Schleswig behind, he and his wife and two small children packed up all their belongings and emigrated to New Holstein, where he decided to become a farmer. In the long run, however, this turned out not to be the right thing for him, since he apparently knew very little about agriculture and had several harvests destroyed by hail. And so he returned to the profession he had learned in Schleswig and opened a butcher shop.

Vollstedt liked to paint in his free time, and could frequently be found out in nature with his brushes and easel. His art became popular among the residents of New Holstein, and Indians in the area also turned out to be great fans. For them, painting the face and the body was a distinct ritual that served as a unique way of decorating the body and as a kind of symbolic language as well. The colors were painted for festivals, wars, or for protection against spirits, with red being the color of Mother Earth and therefore sacred. Finding their array of bodily colors both beautiful and significant, the Indians often went to Nikolaus Vollstedt's butcher shop and had themselves painted.

A Flourishing Economy

Rudolf Puchner had made a good beginning with his general store. As time went on, other companies were founded by the Schleswig-Holstein settlers. Industrial activity began with the construction of a sawmill by the immigrant Joachim Schildhauer from the vicinity of Schleswig. This "lumber baron" supplied materials to the inhabitants of New Holstein and to many of the other people in the surrounding area. His business was followed by factories producing furniture (1859), machinery (1867), cigars (1890), and canned food (1899). Even after the turn of the century, only four of the major entrepreneurs had English names.

Facility with English

Very few of the new settlers spoke English when they arrived in New Holstein, and some never learned more than a few English phrases in their whole lifetime. To the west of Lake Michigan, a self-contained German-language island of about 70 square miles developed.

The first school in New Holstein, later called simply School No. 1, was founded in 1849 and the schoolhouse itself was built two months later. The first teacher was Charles White. He was no stranger to the residents, since he and Wilhelm Ostenfeld had gone to Schleswig-Holstein in 1847 to recruit new settlers. In this way the tension between "the world at home" and "the outside world" was delicately resolved. On the other hand, the teachers who brandished their canes at school in the next few years were mostly Schleswig-Holsteiners who had been trained as teachers in Germany. For this reason it is highly questionable whether English was the universal language of instruction in those early years.

In 1846 a decree was issued in Wisconsin requiring that English be taught in schools. Eight years later this order was intensified into a law stating that all school instruction had to be in English. There was no resistance from the German side. People obeyed authority—and contented themselves with building private schools, which were not affected by the law.

Escaping the Prussians

After 1860, a different type of immigrant began coming to Wisconsin and New Holstein. In only a few cases were they farmers in search of land. They were mostly manual and service workers and had scarcely anything in common with the early settlers. These new settlers were either looking for economic improvement or seeking to escape the mandatory military service that had been introduced in Schleswig-Holstein by the despised Prussians in 1867.

The so-called late immigrants played no significant role at this time in the history of the town, the population of which had by now grown to 1,123. They had no decisive influence in either political or cultural life. Until well into the twentieth century the ruling classes were limited to the children and grandchildren of the first settlers.

German from the Pulpit

Even by the turn of the century, the local pastors still accommodated those few New Holsteiners who could not speak English, though this came to an end after 1920. Confirmation classes were held in the German language until 1908. It was like in the old country: the children had to learn the catechism and sing songs such as "Gott ist die Liebe" (God is love) and "Jesus liebt mich, das weiß ich" (Jesus loves me, this I know).

The first church in New Holstein was built in 1865, eight years after the founding of the Lutheran Society. Participation in church services at that time was quite limited. Only seven families attended, so that the pastor had to expand his duties to other parishes as well. Today's residents of New Holstein, by contrast, have at their disposal six churches of different denominations.

The Advantages of Speaking German

Those who spoke German definitely had an advantage, and business people were well aware of this. Sometimes they put signs saying "German spoken here" in their shop windows. In Holstein, Iowa, an Irish auctioneer even went so far as to learn Low German to help his business. Another curiosity appeared in the advertising section of the *Kiel National-Zeitung*, according to which New Holstein had not only a dentist and a general practitioner, but also a German doctor.

While the children in town mostly grew up speaking both languages, this was not the case on the farms located on the outskirts, since the farm children had little connection with the rest of the world. The contrast between town and country meant that farm children did not come into contact with the English language until they began attending school.

But as time went by, English was spoken by more and more families. When the previously mentioned Nikolaus Vollstedt died, the pastor conducted the funeral oration in English. On December 20, 1900, the *Kiel National-Zeitung* referred to linguistic insufficiencies in its critique of a theater performance of New Holstein's Literary Society: "The plays *Der liederliche Student* (The Dissolute Student) and *A Woman's Trouble* were the main attraction. The English play in particular was well-performed, but it was apparent that the language of the German play caused the actors some difficulties."

In 1914 the *Calumet County Reporter* suggested that farmers name their enterprises. Of the ninety-seven that were suggested, all were in English; there were no German names, and certainly none of Schleswig-Holstein origin.

Language Difficulties on Arrival

The integration of German immigrants was not as quick and easy in other locations as it was in New Holstein. In many places the leap across the Atlantic was fraught with difficulties. In the middle of the eighteenth century, Germans in Pennsylvania refused to allow their children to attend English-language schools; they were not prepared to accept such an intrusion into their private lives. The government and the church reacted to this refusal to integrate with severe measures. They demanded compulsory marriages and a ban on the use of the German language in public. There were anti-German attacks on August 6, 1855 in Louisville, Kentucky, causing twenty-two deaths. Much of the unrest stemmed from religious principles, such as when Germans transgressed against Sunday blue laws.

In order to enforce these laws, the mayor of the ultraconservative "American Party" in Chicago increased the alcohol tax by six hundred percent. When the police raided public houses on Sunday, April 21, 1855 and arrested close to two hundred German guests and several innkeepers for violating the law, the Germans rebelled. The "beer riots," as they were termed in the records, resulted in injuries and at least one death, as the police fired into the angry crowd and shots were fired back.

By contrast, the German immigrants from 1848 and 1849 were fortunate enough in many regions not to be discriminated against. In Texas, for example, they were accepted because of their agricultural techniques and their industriousness, and fit into American society with increasing ease. It is true, however, that unlike the Anglo-American farmers, they employed mostly free laborers in their cotton fields, and this was not viewed with complete sympathy.

Many of the later immigrants still had distinct memories of the wars in their homeland, against Denmark from 1848 to 1851 and in 1864, as well as against France in 1870-71. In 1900, a veterans' society was founded in New Holstein's neighboring town of Kiel, where the local *National-Zeitung* published the following emotional appeal on August 16: "Since so many Germans live here who gave the best years of their lives serving their old fatherland, it would certainly be seen positively for comrades to unite and establish a German veterans' society here as well ... onwards, comrades, you are completely justified in your pride of having once been German soldiers."

In New Holstein, however, there never were such aspirations. Its residents looked to the future, rather than to the past. Immigrants from the south German areas had the reputation of being conservative, while those from the north German coasts were considered liberal-minded. Most New Holsteiners, then, wanted to become American as quickly as possible. As a rule, there was scarcely a year between their arrival and their application for citizenship.

Today New Holstein has about 3,300 inhabitants. Their national origins are overwhelmingly German (73.6%), followed by Polish (8%), Irish (7%), English (4.3%), and Swedish (3.2%).

Chapter 3

The Best of Two Worlds

O f all the possible seasons, why is it that my wife Gitta and I spend our winters in the far-northern state of Minnesota, and our summers in Flensburg? Yes, winter in Minnesota can be bitterly cold at times, but usually the sky is bright blue due to the continental climate, and extreme precipitation is the exception. And then, of course, there is also autumn, with its enchanting "Indian summer" and splendid blaze of colors. This most beautiful season, from September until the beginning of November, is typified by its painter's palette of colors, with every nuance from green to yellow, orange to blood-red, often combined on a single tree.

We look forward to Northfield immensely when we're in Flensburg, and vice versa when we're living in Minnesota. In other words, we try to find the best, the most beautiful, in both worlds. Bad times are put out of mind. We would no more want to do without Schleswig-Holstein, the land between two seas, than we would the invigorating Midwest. Flensburg is magical, but still: when we climbed out of our jetliner in Minneapolis in December 2015, it felt to us like liberation. Away from the confines of densely-populated Germany, back to the vastness of America. But even at that moment we had an inkling of the joy we would feel six months later—as we had for most of the last quarter-century—when we headed back to Old Germany. *The Best of Two Worlds.*

In God's Own Country

Northfield, Minnesota, a town of only 20,000 inhabitants, is home to fifteen churches representing a variety of Christian denominations. The town can be seen as typical of the deep roots of Christian belief in the Midwest. In its own way, the promise made by Frederick the Great more than two hundred years ago to his subjects in Prussia is a reality here: "In my kingdom, everyone can attain salvation according to his own preference."

The liturgy of Lutheran services in the United States is most readily comparable to the traditional German mass. Communion is celebrated every Sunday—with bits of bread in the place of Communion wafers. German visitors experience something of a surprise when they hear "the holy Catholic church" mentioned in the Creed. This, however, is not a reference to the Roman Church, but to an all-encompassing Christian community.

Churches here are characterized by seemingly contradictory basic attitudes. Alongside a deep piety there is an insistence on freedom of belief and the personal control of one's activity in the religious community. To this belong a strong sense of volunteerism and intensive work with young people. Being completely independent of the state, the financial basis for pastoral duties and societal involvement are borne by generous private contributions.

Pastors do not hesitate to proclaim the independence of Christians during presidential elections. Pastor Joseph G. Crippen of St. John's Lutheran Church in Northfield, for example, emphasizes that believers can decide in their own conscience for one candidate or the other. Politicians should not presume to claim that they alone know the true Christian path.

The Roots of Faith

Many of the members of the four Lutheran congregations in Northfield are of German or Scandinavian stock. Individuals of British background are often Congregationalists or Methodists, and the Catholic tradition here was established mostly by Irish and South German immigrants. Regular services, Christian and otherwise, are also offered in Northfield by Quakers, Episcopalians, Baptists, Mennonites, Jehovah's Witnesses, Unitarians, and Buddhists. Ecumenical services sometimes take place in the case of special events.

The Church as a Source of Strength

The irrepressible pioneer spirit and extraordinary hospitality experienced in the small town and rural areas of the Midwest make a deep impression on our German guests from Schleswig-Holstein. In spite of the tremendous growth of the digital revolution, the old social forces of family and church have maintained their function unadulterated. Away from the giant metropolises, there is more than just the striving for success as embodied in the old saying "everyone is the architect of his own fortune"; the principle of brotherly love is also firmly anchored in society here.

Most North German immigrants to the Midwest were Lutheran, and their descendants remain actively involved in living and demonstrating their faith today. In our well-attended church not far from our house in Northfield there is an almost two-hour service every Sunday, including Communion and a Children's Service. In the extensive common room, hundreds of believers gather on weekends for prayer and conversation in a friendly atmosphere.

In addition to the large nave there are numerous side rooms—for the pastors and administration, for small services and Sunday school, for a library, a small museum, and the meetings of active welfare organizations. This forms an impressive building complex that in Schleswig-Holstein could be filled with such active life only in a very large church district. On Sunday most families attend church. The faith of our ancestors has not been lost in the twelve states that make up the Midwest of the United States; it could not be lost, because social processes often of a secular nature were not able to suppress Christian dynamism in those broad expanses of land.

"Divine Providence" and the Forty-Eighters

Even the liberal-minded republicans who emigrated from Schleswig-Holstein following the revolution of 1848-1851 were not able to neutralize such a pronounced belief in God. These political activists, who had experienced a state church in their homeland that was beholden to the secular authorities, generally had no church affiliation of their own. The nineteenth-century pastors in the duchies of Schleswig and Holstein were government officials, and as such dependent on the Danish king, to whom they had sworn allegiance. Whether they wanted to or not, they had to read out political messages emanating from Copenhagen in their sermons. No less a person than the well-known Kiel pastor and provost Claus Harms had turned to the government in the years before the revolution of 1848 in order to denounce the meetings held by the early democratic revolutionary Uwe Jens Lornsen and his associates. The absolutist clergy and the revolutionary-minded citizenry of Schleswig-Holstein had clearly drifted apart in the years after 1830.

Following the defeat of the Schleswig-Holstein revolutionaries by Denmark in 1850, the Forty-Eighters who had come to the Midwest promoted non-denominational religion. They founded gymnastic and choral societies and sought, with the help of their German-language newspapers, to win over the populace to their ideals of freedom and justice. A belief in God as the final authority for ethical responsibility had increasingly dwindled away. Democratic revolution and the fight against slavery and bondage were for them the path that free citizens had to take toward the goal of a better world. In place of a God who demanded belief and piety, there was more and more talk of "providence," an otherworldly power that no longer had the contours of the authoritarian Christian image of God that the Forty-Eighters had experienced themselves and had criticized.

But in the great expanses of the Midwest such rhetoric and its goals could not be met with complete success. Taking possession of this virtually endless land could be understood as a God-given bestowal as in the Old Testament. More pointedly, communities with Anglo-Saxon roots could look back on the long tradition of a religious struggle for freedom that originated with the founding of the Anglican Church as it broke with the Roman Catholic Church. The Schleswig-Holstein political activists came to the realization that Christian faith and liberal convictions were not mutually exclusive in their newly-established frontier society.

Collective Spirituality Following my Wife's Automobile Accident

Here in the Midwest, the church is still experienced as an extended family—a bonding of congregants offering mutual help, united through creed and hymn, prayer and offertory. Belief is not an exclusively private matter here, it is important for life in and with the community. My wife Gitta and I experienced directly what significance this can have in one's everyday life.

Gitta and I had been a couple since the early 1990s. In 1992, when I began teaching at St. Olaf College in Northfield, we began what was to become our pattern of living six months of the year there and the other six months in Flensburg. Three years later, on Thanksgiving Day 1995, I had just given a lecture at the German Embassy in Washington when an acquaintance asked me why Gitta and I were still single. This innocently-asked question had an immediate effect; only a few days later she and I flew to Las Vegas and were married there on November 27.

Only four months after that, on March 30, 1996, I stood anxiously in the waiting room of the hospital in Sioux City, Iowa. Gitta and I had been traveling in Iowa, in separate vehicles, for the purpose of giving several German politicians an idea of Midwestern farming practices. Gitta had been in a horrendous automobile accident on an icy road and was fighting for her life in a nearby operating room. After a four-weeks' stay in the intensive-care unit, I had Gitta taken to the Mayo Clinic, where she was in the care of the best doctors I could ever imagine, Gene Keller and Bob DePompolo. John Gorder, an administrator and pastor at St. Olaf College, arrived on the spot to care for Gitta, to pray for her and for us. At the time, the church bells of Northfield rang out—a sign to this deeply religious community that someone was in need, in need of prayers and possibly of material help as well. What those church bells meant to her despondent husband can scarcely be expressed in words.

Behind this experience there stands a robust Christian faith that does not offer empty phrases, but spiritual community and human consideration. And this can happen anytime, on the spur of the moment, without great pronouncements, taking the form in which church and Christianity, even now in the twenty-first century, have in no way been lost in the American Midwest.

Gitta and her indomitable spirit have survived. Over twenty years later, though both physically and mentally impaired, she continues to take small steps toward recovery and is still able to understand both German and English. Among the phrases she often says is her clear favorite: an enthusiastic "I live!"

1997: Gitta's 50. birthday in Northfield, MN.

Chapter 4

Not Getting Up Again
is a Weakness

The Journalist Dieter E. Wilhelmy

interviews Joachim "Yogi" Reppmann

Dieter: Is there such a thing as an American mentality?

Yogi: I find it difficult to describe what might be called "American mentality," just as it is difficult to formulate a sweeping description of what "German" is. But there is a kind of temperamental memory in social groups that we perceive as "typically German" or "typically American," although this does not exist as a closed system of national characteristics. America is certainly full of contradictions. But there is a difference here in mentality when compared with the "Old World." These contradictions are not perceived as shortcomings, and there is no attempt to resolve them. In America they are considered a source of progress instead.

Germans who visit America, but also Americans or immigrants who return to Germany, experience a striking difference: Americans predominantly look forward to the future. They ask themselves and others: What is the next step? How can we make this better? Conversations and questionnaires in Germany reveal quite a different picture. The future makes us fearful; the status quo seems to give us security. Many things create fear, such as a past that has not been dealt with, or a future that is uncertain.

Dieter: There is hardly another people who has as much difficulty as we Germans do in accepting ourselves. The family therapist Gabriele Baring believes that there is more than just a collective disorder in the lack of well-being we sense; she sees its causes in the areas of emotional life that we have inherited and accepted. Because we are unconsciously connected to what happened to those who preceded us, we are shaped even today by the horrors of the past century, which continue to affect us in the form of shame and guilt feelings.

Yogi: True, Americans don't get hung up on the past. They say "falling down isn't disgraceful, but not getting up again is a weakness!" The Austrian film director Billy Wilder made this positive attitude into a tenet of filmmaking: "The difference between a comedy and a tragedy is: a man runs along a street and falls down. If he gets up again, it's a comedy, and people laugh; if he stays on the ground, it's a tragedy." This is a perfect description of the American spirit. Get up again, continue what you were doing.

Dieter: Why have the "old" and the "new" world drifted so far apart?

Yogi: America's history is a history of success. Believing in success has also produced success—sort of a different take of the notion of a "self-fulfilling prophecy." The person who believes in himself has a better chance of winning. Of course mistakes have been made and still are in America, no less or no more than anywhere else. But inferences drawn from these are different. Before tearing yourself apart in self-doubt and self-pity, you repair the broken wagon wheel, tighten it on the axle, and the cart is ready to go again.

Dieter: So it's clearly not only the sense of well-being that makes us different, it's also planning and taking action.

Yogi: Germans set themselves a goal and follow it closely. This sounds positive and does function well with large-scale tasks. But it blocks alternative, divergent ways of thinking and finding new ideas "on the road." When a German goes on a trip, he has planned the route carefully, booked his hotel in advance, and calculated his arrival time. An American gets into his car, drives off, and enjoys the surprises along the way. This is precisely how new ideas are born, projects developed, and useful products invented. They're not always perfect, but they're creative.

Dieter: But this way of doing things can't be innate?

Yogi: Of course not. This kind of thinking is furthered at a very early age. While German children are supposed to be sent along the "right path," different paths are pointed out to American children and they're allowed to experiment. They're especially encouraged to try things, to accumulate new experiences, but to be kind to those around them as well.

Dieter: The attitude of Americans that is conveyed by the media, and especially by certain films, is characterized by egotism, impolite manners in the workplace, and brutality on the streets. That isn't how being kind to others should look . . .

Yogi: My wife and I have had experiences that have been just the opposite. And not only after her automobile accident, when we experienced enormous caring and people willing to offer personal help.

There is an immense willingness to help among Americans in general. This is also apparent on a small scale, in individual gift-giving, which is much more prevalent than in Germany. For a successful American it's automatic to let other people share in his success, to give back what society has made possible for him. On a grand scale, Bill Gates and his wife Melinda maintain a foundation that has at its disposal estimated assets of close to 40 billion dollars. To date, the fund has donated around 7.5 billion for charitable purposes, mostly to provide vaccines and additional health projects in developing countries in Africa and Asia.

The result is that Gates has returned almost one-quarter of his assets to "global society." This is not an isolated case in the United States. Warren Buffett, the joyful multi-billionaire and stock market oracle from Omaha, Nebraska has given ninety percent of his fortune to the Gates Foundation and motivated forty-two other American billionaires (as well as Hasso Plattner, the founder of the German software firm SAP) to donate gigantic amounts (a minimum of one billion dollars).

Dieter: Fine, that certainly has a lot of public appeal. But are ordinary people really as free in making contributions?

Yogi: Dieter, let me tell you a story: We had a cleaning lady who lives in very modest circumstances, definitely not part of the privileged classes. In the first Obama campaign for president she gave three dollars a month for almost two years. Three million American citizens did the same thing at that time. And there wasn't any BMW as grand prize.

Dieter: The question is, is that consistent with the frequently-cited American individualism? You gave me a book by the writer and philosopher Walt Whitman. In 1868, shortly after the end of the Civil War that was so decisive for the subsequent development of America, he wrote of the importance of individualism in American democracy. Isn't that a contradiction to what you just described?

Yogi: No. Individualism isn't the same as egotism. Americans don't wait until state institutions resolve some societal problem or other in the private sphere. They actually even resist the wielding of power by the state. Rather than that, they try to help on the level of the people through collective action, for example with neighborhood assistance. The community plays a major role here.

Dieter: So in Germany we have a different idea of social responsibility and individualism. The understanding of democracy in Europe was strongly influenced by the socialist workers' movement after the defeat of the middle-class revolution of 1848. The individual has his personal demands represented by the collective (unions, associations, parties). That led to the growth of "representative politics" in Europe. The middle-class Christian parties adopted the principle in the concept of "social market economy." Individual striving for prosperity, yes, but assuming responsibility for the community as well ("ownership is an obligation"). In the course of this development, in spite of the emphasis on individual rights of freedom, the degree of state regulation and maintenance increased. Social services, for example, are not a "gift" of society, but a legally guaranteed right.

Yogi: It was precisely in this formative period that American history took a different course. In America social responsibility is seen more as a duty of society than of the state. President Obama's struggle for a health care system safeguarded by the state and the massive resistance to it make this evident. Individual responsibility takes precedence. Assistance by the community, but not by the state. This is not only taught to children, it runs through all the stages of American education. An application to study at a college, often financed by scholarships, calls for "social skills"—characteristically seen in Germany as "soft" factors. Social involvement and volunteer work has merit in the States and is seen as an advantage that can be decisive for acceptance by a college.

Dieter: What we Germans find disconcerting is the blatant patriotism of Americans.

Yogi: Yes, Americans have a distinct loyalty to their constitution. This involves various rituals, such as waving the flag on any occasion and singing the national anthem. Still, it is not nationalism. The flag isn't displayed to enemies, but to the immigrants and their descendants as a symbol of the fusion of peoples, a declaration of American identity. It is a kind of dramatization of a new beginning, setting out for new shores, the "new frontier"— ultimately a symbol of the American Dream.

Dieter: In the 1860s, Walt Whitman thought he had discovered in the American citizen an unrestrained evolutionary power that would surpass old Europe culturally as well. Has he proven to be right?

Yogi: Definitely. Whitman was simply an American, through and through. His belief in the strength of the nation, which would make anything possible, was symptomatic. Especially concerning the music of the next century and the one after that, he was certainly right.

Dieter: Well, maybe as far as the art of music for entertainment is concerned . . .

Yogi: This differentiation between serious music and music for entertainment is, again, typical of Europe, and especially of Germans. In America the transition from "serious" music and music for entertainment is fluid. Jazz, gospel music, blues, and the rock music that was derived from it are characteristic of music today, and not only in the youth scene. Igor Stravinsky, for example, appropriated elements of jazz in his "serious music." Gershwin lived at the beginning of the last century. Symphonic jazz—give it a try! Different styles get mixed and create new ones. That again is typically American. And the "Old World" absorbed it eagerly, actually even before the war and the period of occupation. Today it's known as "crossover." Classical orchestras play pop music, jazz musicians play classical music. This unbiased experimentation, this liberation from genre categories, is characteristic of American art, too. Andy Warhol, who was actually a classically-trained graphic artist, introduced new trends, dissolving the boundaries between painting, drawing, and photography. America was, and is, a gigantic laboratory of ideas, experiments, and new products.

Dieter: Thank you for the interview, Yogi. I have acquired a new image of America, a country that was, admittedly, quite unknown to me previously.

Chapter 5

Yogi's Friends
German-American Perspectives

Erhard "Boeddee" Böttcher

My friend Boeddee likes to joke with me about "those superficial Americans"—a seemingly common prejudgment among Germans. He'll say to me ironically, for instance: "Look over there—more of those superficial Americans." And my wife Gitta, who has experienced the States intimately for thirty years herself, will grin along with us. In spite of being severely handicapped as a result of an automobile accident, she sees into the human heart with her clear sensibility more deeply than many an able-bodied intellectual. The point is, any person who has not lived among Americans, made friends with them, gotten to know them as neighbors through thick and thin—that person ought not to rush to what will probably be an inaccurate judgment.

To date, Boeddee has participated in seven event-filled study trips to the United States totaling approximately thirty-five months. Among the characteristics of Americans that he treasures in particular are their sensitivity, humor, generosity, and straightforwardness. They find it easy to put themselves at a new visitor's disposal, without setting aside their accustomed daily rhythm. On one occasion, his German-American host Roger Clausen, a furniture manufacturer, casually handed him the keys to his brand-new BMW with the off-hand suggestion that he might drive on ahead, since he still had a few things to take care of in his office. In a similar situation, a woman of Irish background named Margaret McGuire suggested that he should make himself at home in her place and help himself to the contents of her abundantly stocked refrigerator while she went to visit a girlfriend.

And Boeddee experienced other instances of American helpfulness while traveling in the United States: there was the taxi driver in Washington, D.C. who was willing to accept payment in stamps when it turned out that their passengers (Boeddee and his pregnant wife) had not brought enough cash along; or the semi-driver with a load of squealing pigs who towed his car, with its failed battery, to a gas station and waited in the extreme heat until he was sure that Boeddee had gotten through to a repair service.

My friend found Christmastime in America to be an especially joyous occasion. As a visitor from Europe, he was surprised at first when helpful neighbors rang the doorbell every other afternoon, bringing homemade cakes and jams, and fish they'd caught themselves (yes, even in the middle of winter!). Cookies were sampled, recipes exchanged, a glass of beer or wine was offered, and in heart-felt conversations everything under the sun was discussed. Given all this depth of genuine feeling . . . is there anyone who would make the accusation of superficiality now?!

Four generations of the Böttcher family: Ricarda,
Elsbeth, Laura, and Erhard.

Virginia Degen

It's difficult to imagine the tiny, delicate woman with the curly white hair and smiling eyes amidst a bunch of grunting hogs. But for decades, Virginia Degen was the mistress of more than two thousand such creatures on the thriving hog farm that she and her husband Leonard founded in Holstein, Iowa. And thanks to Virginia's indefatigable efforts over three decades, about five hundred visitors from Schleswig-Holstein have come to know this tiny spot in America's heartland. More importantly, because of this energetic and remarkable woman an intense transatlantic friendship between Holstein, Iowa and Schleswig-Holstein in Germany grew and prospered.

The seeds for this extraordinary friendship were sown in 1978, when my fellow Kiel University friend Dietrich "Dee" Eicke and I journeyed to America to research German immigration to the United States. Our bright idea of visiting American towns with German names brought us to Holstein, Iowa, and it was there that we met Virginia Degen. Our shared love of history led us to try and better understand the Germanic roots of this small Midwestern town. Among other things, we learned the curious fact that the founder of the town, Joachim Thode, had not named it after the Duchy of Holstein, but after New Holstein, Wisconsin, where he had grown up!

Dee and I were treated like royalty during our stay in Holstein. When we left to return to Germany, we invited Virginia and all her fellow Holstein residents to come visit us there. Little did we know at the time that this invitation would become the first pier in a transatlantic bridge that would carry the traffic of countless visits. That summer, the Degens arrived in Germany accompanied by forty-two farmers who hoped to experience the landscape of Schleswig-Holstein and to travel to other parts of Germany as well. During a week-long stay in Schleswig-Holstein, hosts and guests alike were amazed that they were able to communicate about their farming experiences in the local Plattdeutsch dialect. This discovery was a great joy to both the Germans and the visiting Americans.

Since those early years, Schleswig-Holstein musicians, politicians, and even German parliament members made their way to the tiny town of Holstein and its one-woman welcome wagon. In turn, Virginia became a regular visitor to Schleswig-Holstein.

Virginia Degen—a certified Braille transcriber for almost thirty years and the co-author of *Building a Bridge*, about reestablishing contacts with the ancestral homeland—died in 2015 at the age of 91. At the Northfield Conference 2017, we inaugurated *The Virginia Degen Lecture Series* in German-American Studies in memory of her transatlantic bridge-building.

Top: 1982: Holstein Centennial parade, enjoying a ride in a Cadillac Eldorado.
Bottom: 1982: Yogi (left) and Dee (right) back in their German student apartment where a gift from the Holstein Centennial Committee, an Iowa flag, hangs.

Merl Arp

I first met Merl Arp, an American career diplomat, nearly thirty years ago in Bad Segeberg in Schleswig-Holstein. At least that was the first time I met Merl in person. Because my friend Holger Anderson from Kiel (a Forty-Eighter expert and author of the historical account *Idstedt und danach*) had spoken so often about his friend, I felt as if I knew Merl before I'd even met him.

During that first meeting I peppered Merl with an endless stream of questions and ideas, all relating to what we could do to foster a special friendship between my home state of Schleswig-Holstein and America. It became obvious that Merl was open to any suggestions that might strengthen the bonds between his ancestral homeland (some of his ancestors hailed from the Probstei region, near Kiel) and the United States.

Emboldened by his interest, I informed him of my plans for a group tour of north Germans ("On the trail of the Schleswig-Holstein immigrants in America") that was to take place a few months later, in 1988. I asked Merl whether he would be able to lend support for the tour. After informing me that he would be retiring near Washington, D.C. in a few weeks, he surprised me by turning the tables and asking: "Yogi, might I volunteer to assist with the sightseeing activities of your group in Washington?" Needless to say, I was dumbstruck.

Merl not only accompanied our group of north Germans in Washington, but also accepted our invitation to join the group at the end of the tour in Davenport, Iowa—which, as luck would have it, was his hometown. On short notice, he booked a flight and met us there. All the group members were enchanted by Merl's dynamic and charismatic personality. My hard-to-please mother, who had come along on the trip, confided to me that Merl was "the best-looking American I have ever met or will ever meet."

While attending a party in Scott County Park, Merl and I continued the discussion we had begun in Bad Segeberg about founding the organization that became known as ASHHS, the *American/Schleswig-Holstein Heritage Society*. Our dream became reality in early January of 1989. Before long Merl volunteered to be editor of the society's newsletter, penning articles that were consistently well-researched and informative. Five years after the founding of ASHHS, Merl and my father led a group of German visitors to our very first Forty-Eighter conference and Claussen centennial celebration: "The Legacy of 1848: Trailblazers of Democracy." Once again, Merl charmed the German guests with his charisma and sense of humor.

Merl Arp died in 2016 at the age of 84. He had an illustrious career in the foreign service and there can be no doubt that he did more than his share in helping to maintain and improve German-American relations.

Roscoe Hall, near downtown Chicago, where the Schleswig-Holstein Choir was founded in 1881.

Evelyn Sadri

Evelyn, our Flensburg neighbor—she literally lives right next door—is a true friend, one who is always willing to help, whether as our Flensburg "secretary" while we are living on the other side of the Atlantic, or during her welcome visits to us in Northfield. Evelyn has had to struggle through life on many occasions, including surviving two difficult, but necessary divorces. But she is a person—to paraphrase Billy Wilder—who always gets up again when she is down, and continues on her way with courage, self-confidence, and good-humor. Anyone who meets her is struck by her aura of humility and contentment.

Along with raising four highly talented children, Evelyn worked for twenty years side-by-side with a dedicated physician who treated drug addicts. On returning home to Flensburg following a year-long bout with a pernicious case of cancer, she did not simply settle in for her well-deserved rest, but instead became the indispensable heart and soul of the Reppmann household, managing all the necessities during our absence. This includes taking charge of our not-so-small "post office," sending books, letters, and cards all over the world and keeping the place in perfect order. From time to time she welcomes and cooks for American visitors. On one unusual occasion, she dramatically showed her undaunted strength of character, when my presumptuous brother's family tried to catch her unawares and gain access to our apartment without permission. Evelyn kept her cool in the entryway and on the street, hung onto the keys, and sent the familial aggressors on their way.

Our friend has not, of course, stayed on our home grounds in Flensburg continuously as our tried and true housemother, since the adventurous part of her likes to get to know other places as well, both in Germany and abroad. In 2016, during two wonderful four-week stays in Northfield, Evelyn grew spontaneously enthusiastic about our American Way of Life. Whenever she wasn't otherwise occupied, she enjoyed strolling around Northfield on her own and getting to know what a small American town is like. She met several of our friends and even prepared Schnitzel and German noodles for them on at least one occasion. During Gitta's "round" birthday celebration, to which over one hundred people were invited, her assistance in helping to make sure that things went smoothly was essential. On an everyday basis, too, her caring nature was evident when it came to seeing to Gitta's needs.

Evelyn was in Northfield again, for our 2017 Forty-Eighter conference in March/April and to help celebrate another "round" birthday—in this instance, my own! As always, she will be a most welcome guest.

January 12th, 2017: Evelyn Sadri and Erna de Vries,
Auschwitz survivor, in front of the Flensburg
Police Headquarters. See Appendix 4, p. 90.

Eric Braeden

The well-known film, theater, and television actor Eric Braeden (born in Schleswig-Holstein as Hans-Jörg Gudegast) emigrated to the United States at the age of eighteen. At our 48er conference in Denison, Iowa in 2009, Eric gave a stimulating talk about his sense of being a German and about changing American attitudes toward Germans in the decades following the war:

I remember going to the university in Montana, and one day in a lecture on philosophy being asked in front of the whole class, how it was possible that a country that had produced Goethe and Schiller and Beethoven and Schubert could produce Hitler and concentration camps? I was eighteen then, and couldn't answer.

I remember fighting with producers on how to play my role in the *Rat Patrol*. They wanted an eyepatch and a limp so as to perpetuate the stereotypical image of a German soldier. And I insisted on playing the Rommel-like figure as a human being, with dignity, because the German soldier of the Afrika Korps who came back from the blood-drenched vastness of the Sahara Desert was decent and brave and tough and fought for his country just like any other soldier.

I remember my son coming home from grade school one day and telling me that he had been called a Nazi, and asking me what that meant, and I remember my trying to explain something I had taken years to study and understand.

Then, in 1989, the Berlin Wall came down and Americans congratulated me and it felt good to be German. And then came some editorials in the newspapers about the renaissance of German power and a caricature of Helmut Kohl as a new Hitler.

As a German, I wanted to shout to the world: When will you ever give us credit for more than sixty peaceful democratic years during which Germany has been an exemplary democracy, a country that has opened its arms to more politically disenfranchised, the persecuted and hungry, than any other except perhaps America? When will you ever acknowledge the untold contributions made by German immigrants who toiled for you, America, as carpenters, farmers, mechanics, longshoremen, doctors and nurses, coal miners, lawyers, surgeons, generals and presidents, teachers and scientists?

It will happen when we German immigrants and Americans of German descent have dialogue with those who mistrust us and who were wronged by another generation, when we become aware of our profound contributions to the success in freedom and democracy that is America.

When I reflect upon Germany, I am proud of what it has accomplished in the last seventy years. It has risen from the ashes of World War II, it has passionately pursued a rapprochement with all its neighbors since 1949, so that together they could form a united Europe without the paroxysms of devastating wars, without borders and ethnic divisions, a Europe that is finally anchored in shared democratic values.

Eric Braeden and Gitta Reppmann, Santa Monica, CA, 1999. When Eric takes my spouse out for dinner to his favorite Italian Restaurant, they tell me to enjoy myself at the nearest hamburger diner. Eric Braeden and Gitta Reppmann in Santa Monica, CA. Eric lives in Pacific Palisades, CA, known as "Weimar am Pazifik" since 1933; across from his house is the elegant villa where Thomas Mann, a German literature Nobel laureate from Schleswig-Holstein, spent his years in exile during the Second World War. Braeden has appeared in over 120 TV productions and films, including "Titanic" (1997). Beginning in 1980, he has made daily appearances on US TV, as well as in 28 other countries world-wide with "The Young and the Restless," and in 1989 he founded the "German-American Cultural Society." In 2007, Eric became only the second German actor (after Marlene Dietrich) to receive a Star in the Hollywood Walk of Fame.

Eric Braeden
From Bredenbek to Hollywood: The Legacy of 1848, Through Today

Eric Braeden

**From Bredenbek to Hollywood:
The Legacy of 1848, Through Today**

moin
moin

Joachim Reppmann and Erhard Böttcher, Editors

Although only a very young child at the time, Braeden has vivid recollections of World War II's horrors. Nearby Kiel was one of the major naval bases and shipbuilding centers of the German Reich. - In 2005, he joined Ariel Sharon, Elie Wiesel, the prime ministers of Poland and Hungary, and twenty thousand Christians and Jews for "The March of the Living," an annual memorial march from Auschwitz to Birkenau. - Eric has also been invited to speak in Israel on several occasions by former Prime Minister Sharon and late President Shimon Peres. Eric and Yogi are fascinated by the timeless concepts, ideas and values of a democratic revolution, The Legacy of 1848.

Book order: www.LuLu.com - Printing on Demand: Eric Braeden, From Bredenbek to Hollywood, by Joachim Reppmann and Erhard Böttcher, Editors.

I'll be Damned
Eric Braeden

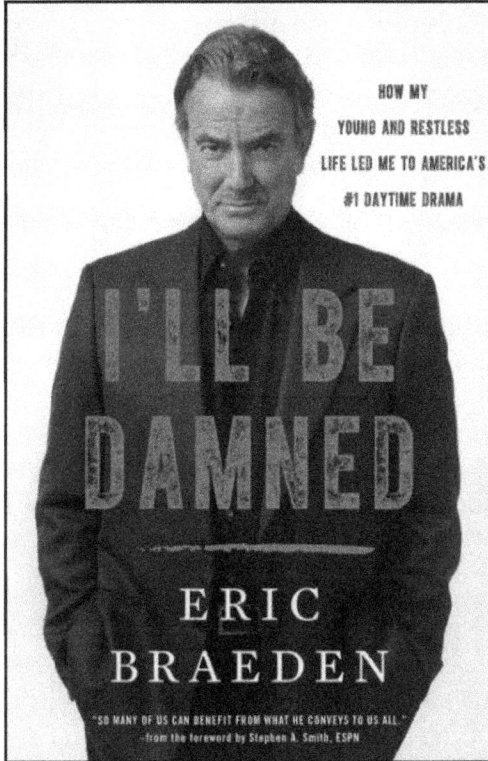

In this startling candid and poignant memoir, the legendary Emmy Award-winning star chronicles his amazing life, from his birth in WWII Germany to his arrival in America. Braeden's journey from a hospital basement in Kiel to the sound stages of Los Angeles has taught him more about joy, heartbreak, fear, dignity, loss, love, loneliness, exhilaration, courage, persecution, and profound responsibility to the global community than he could have hoped to learn in several lifetimes. Growing up in the years after Germany's defeat, Braeden knew very little about the atrocities of his parents' generation, until he arrived in America as a teenager. Trying to redress the wrongs of his homeland, he formed the *German American Culture Society* and has dedicated his life to humanitarian work. For decades he has shown the world that what we share as humans is far more important than what separates us from one another.

Joey Kronzer

My getting to know Joey Kronzer came about in a somewhat unusual way: not as a student at St. Olaf College while I was teaching there, but years later, during a tennis clinic at which he, as a member of the college's tennis team, was one of the student instructors. He seemed to appreciate it when I told him that I enjoyed his teaching style and his passion for the game, and we soon discovered that we shared not only a love for the game of tennis, but that we had many other things in common, including an interest in history, in neuroscience, and in conducting research.

The second semester of Joey's Junior year began soon after our encounter on the tennis court, and he was extremely busy for several weeks. After midterms, though, he emailed me to set up a lunch date and to discuss a possible research project. I was working on several at the time, but the one that caught Joey's eye had to do with creating a bilingual story based on an American couple's experiences at work camps in Germany just after World War II. The young married couple concerned were Ian and Deane Barbour, who happened to be the parents of a current St. Olaf religion professor, John Barbour. Joey did essential work developing the layout of the story, which detailed the daily routine of work camps in Münster and Hamburg with all their successes and disappointments.

Our next collaborative effort was not in the field of research, but took place once again . . . on a tennis court! Remembering Joey's skilful playing, I decided to call my friend and fellow Schleswig-Holsteiner, the Hollywood star Eric Braeden, to set up a doubles match. Joey and I would fly out to California at the end of his spring break to meet our destiny.

We walked onto Court 1 at the Rivera Tennis Club in Pacific Palisades on April 4, 2015 to do battle with Eric and his doubles partner Phillip, a UCLA graduate. As it turned out, we did not mind terribly that we lost rather badly (6-0, 6-0), since it was especially gratifying for Joey to meet Eric Braeden, who, he discovered, was remarkably human and respectful in spite of his dominating presence and fame. Through this encounter, Joey was reminded of the things that truly matter in life: not a big house or fancy cars, but people. He expressed it so well when he said that the relationships one forms with others are the things that have a lasting impact upon more than just oneself. Well on his way to having created lifelong friendships, Joey is fond of speaking of "Eric and Yogi, my two friends from northern Germany."

Stephan Richter and Jim Amoss

In 2005, Stephan Richter was chief editor of the Schleswig-Holstein Newspaper Chain in Flensburg, and Jim Amoss held the same post at the *Times-Picayune* far across the ocean in New Orleans. Jim happened to be completely fluent in German, since he had gone to school in Bremen during his father's military tour of duty in Germany. He later went on to study German literature at Yale and Oxford, specializing in the works of Thomas Mann.

In that same year, 2005, the devastation of Hurricane Katrina struck New Orleans in August, inundating large portions of the city. When Stephan heard about Jim's background in German and in northern Germany, he was so electrified that he contacted me in Minnesota to see about setting up a large-scale relief operation. Readers of the Schleswig-Holstein Newspapers were asked to contribute to help the poorest victims, and they came through with the amazing sum of 160,000 euros. Two friends of mine, Rick Esse and Erhard "Boeddee" Böttcher, drove along the Mississippi with me to the damaged region to discuss the best way of apportioning the money.

Later on, Jim Amoss flew to Germany to attend a thank-you party in Flensburg that was attended by 8,000 people. That was the perfect time to bring the two chief editors together to become friends as well. It is difficult to imagine a better example of cross-Atlantic willingness to help than the spur-of-the-moment fundraising organized by the dedicated editor Stephan Richter between Flensburg and New Orleans.

Through Jim Amoss's efforts, the *Times-Picayune* had already become one of the leading newspapers in the United States. He was named Editor of the Year by the National Press Foundation in 1997, and by Editor and Publisher in 2006, when he also won an award for Editorial Leadership from the American Society of News Editors. In the same year he received a Henri Nannen Prize as well, for his editorial work on the *Times-Picayune*.

The combined efforts of Stephan Richter and Jim Amoss illustrate how two great editors were able to work together to achieve a humanitarian result that affected the lives of thousands.

Dietrich "Dee" Eicke

I first met Dee Eicke in a student pub at the University of Kiel. We soon discovered that we had several things in common. We were both from Schleswig-Holstein, of course, and we had both just started studying history and English—and, even more significantly, we shared the same nickname! As a schoolboy, Dee had occasionally been called "Yogi"; in my case I had been dubbed "Yogi" much earlier, and the nickname has continued to this very day.

Although Dee was especially fond of England (and the Isle of Wight off the Channel coast in particular), he readily agreed during a long conversation that the United States had a certain appeal for us native Schleswig-Holsteiners. My plan was to undertake a research trip to the American Midwest, where many emigrants from our home state had settled in the nineteenth century. We would explore towns with appealing names such as Flensburg in the state of Minnesota, Schleswig and Holstein in Iowa, Kiel and New Holstein in Wisconsin—and on the way there we might even stop at Lubec (minus the umlaut and "k") in the eastern state of Maine!

Dr. Gerhard Stoltenberg, Minister-President of Schleswig-Holstein, convinced of the value of our project (both as part of our own education and for the furthering of German-American relations), graciously agreed to fund our trip. We left for the United States in the fall of 1978 and spent three months investigating the history of those towns and several more, and enjoying the hospitality of countless German-American families.

Then, four years later, Dee and I set out on a six-month study trip to the same area, our goal being to carry out in-depth background research on the history of the Schleswig-Holstein Forty-Eighters for our Master's theses. One of our more memorable experiences took place at the Centennial celebration in Holstein, Iowa, where our hosts were astonished as Dee—himself an excellent gourmet chef—made his way to the salad bar seven times and consumed two entire steak dinners! This was, I believe, a highly successful attempt on Dee's part at furthering German-American relations on one of the most basic human levels! Yes, we certainly had a wonderful time during those six months and were once again treated like royalty by our hosts. Our studies prevailed, however, and we both completed our Master's degrees in 1984, two days before Christmas.

Since then, Dee Eicke has pursued radically different career options. Over a span of thirty years he was a highly successful IT coach, and then, making use of his exceptional speaking skills, he became a professional funeral orator. But his interest in history has remained a constant with him over the years, and it was a pleasure to welcome him to Northfield this spring of 2017 and enjoyed him speak about the Forty-Eighters who settled in one of the towns he and I visited so long ago.

www.trauerredner-eicke.de

Dee Eicke and Bebe Diehl preparing Omaha Steaks.

Friedhelm „Fiede" Caspari

I had just finished my secondary education when this "man from the Mosel" crossed my path. With a bottle of Mosel wine in his hand—an exotic beverage for me, a confirmed beer-drinker—Friedhelm Caspari appeared in April 1976 at a party in Flensburg that friends of mine were giving. At the beginning of March, he had entered the services of the German Press Agency (dpa) as district editor for Schleswig-Holstein North and the German-Danish border region. Thirty years old at the time, he had left his "cold homeland," the Mosel region, because he did not get along with his father, a publisher and printer of a small newspaper. "As far away as possible," was what Fiede wanted, and so he ended up in Flensburg, 800 kilometers away. It was not until he had moved to the North that he was given his Low German nickname, an abbreviated form of Friedrich.

At that point, shortly before I began my studies at the University of Kiel, I had no way of knowing that Fiede would later become an important journalistic companion on my own professional pathways. In the fall of 1988 he became part of the first group trip I organized. Its purpose was to explore the American Midwest, following in the footsteps of Schleswig-Holstein emigrants. Afterwards Fiede wrote enthusiastically about the trip for dpa as well as for the newspaper "Flensborg Avis," the mouthpiece of the Danish minority. Then, in October 1988, Fiede went on to formulate a bold mind game in a travel report: What would be likely to happen if some day Americans decided to leave their country? Would many Americans of German origin—there's said to be about forty million of them today—possibly return to Europe?! In those days, when the end of communism was approaching, Germany admitted a few thousand (no more than that!) ethnic Germans from the Soviet Union. Many of these so-called German Russians still have not been assimilated and live in the larger cities in closed, Russian-language enclaves.

In later years, too, my friend Fiede, with his willingness to listen and his sharp intellect, has always shown great interest in my ideas for symposia and the creation of educational materials, which he is able to disseminate via dpa. Most recently (2015/2016) he came up with the brilliant idea for the "fact book" that have written together: "The Holocaust Boxcar: A Powerful Admonition Against Anti-Semitism," in which the most sinister period of German history is documented and made vivid through the inclusion of personal experiences. (Cf. Appendix 4, page 90) Inevitably, Fiede has splendid ideas to offer, although I have to admit that he sometimes has to slow me down in my boundless enthusiasm—and justifiably so.

Friedhelm (Fiede) Caspari* was born in 1946 near the Mosel River, in the wine region of Rheinland-Pfalz. He has had decades of press and media experience, including as a newspaper editor and as North German correspondent of the German Press Agency (dpa), together from 1968 to 2008. In his current freelance journalistic activities he covers historical topics, biographies, business analyses, and the realm of medicine and pharmacy. - In 1988 he took part in the first in a series of U.S. excursions, organized and led by the historian Dr. Joachim "Yogi" Reppmann, under the title of "On the Trail of the Schleswig-Holstein Immigrants." Highly motivated since that time, Fiede Caspari has followed the German-American involvement of his friend Yogi and has frequently commented on it in his writings. Born immediately after the crushing of the Nazi dictatorship and the end of the Second World War, Fiede Caspari sees it as his self-evident duty to elucidate those horrific years and not let them fade from memory. In the case of most families, the silence that dominated the Nazi generation and the German participants in the war remained unbroken until subsequent generations. - In the present situation, Caspari has increasingly underscored the unmistakable tendencies toward a growing right-wing extremism that has developed not only in Germany but in the rest of Europe and the United States as well. Definite parallels to the unstable years of democracy in Germany after the First World War cannot be overlooked. An outside observer might well say: nip these early signs in the bud—a burning candle can be extinguished, but not a forest fire.

www.caspari-pr.de

*The name "Caspari," of Italian and/or Roman origin, is not unknown in many cities of the United States. It goes back almost 2,000 years to the Romans' foundation of the city of Trier on the Mosel River and other settlements. The original (Catholic) spelling is Caspary, while the later Protestant and Jewish lines use the form Caspari.

Epilogue

American Century

The twentieth century has been called the "American Century," in large part because of the country's essential role in two world wars and its economic successes. The United States had more influence throughout the world in that century than any previous superpower. Almost the entire planet loved huge American automobiles; people revered Hollywood stars, imitated the American way of life, and looked at New York as the capital of the world. Neither the Vietnam War nor the political scandal of Watergate did much to change this view, which was further bolstered by the demise of the Soviet Union in 1991.

The opening decades of the twenty-first century have been a different story. America is facing huge challenges: wars in the Middle East that have spun out of control; the potentially dangerous positions of Russia in Europe and China in the Far East; at home, an increase in gun violence and racial hate crimes; a clash between those who welcome Hispanic workers and refugees from devastated countries, and those who would retreat into self-protective isolationism.

Although no one can predict what the future will hold, it is clear that the presidential elections of 2016 have only added to the polarization of large segments of the population.

Gitta and I are optimistic that America, as always full of contradictions, will be preserved through the self-purifying power of its democracy and emerge stronger. If this happens, there will be the possibility of yet another "American Century," imbued with the values of its founding fathers.

2008: Gitta and Yogi in Froggy Bottoms River Pub in Northfield MN.

Part Two

Appendices

Appendix 1

German vs. American Way of Life

Americans have a way of interacting with others that contrasts starkly with the way we Germans do things. American history is characterized by success stories that grew out of liberal values. In contrast to the situation in Germany, the first Europeans to reach the New World had no ready-made society waiting for them. Europeans became Americans through their individual decision to emigrate. Almost every American family sprang from this act of will.

A collective mentality was formed, at least in part, by the situation that the immigrants found themselves in. There was always a break between the immigrants themselves and their American-born children. These children spoke perfect English while their parents struggled with the new language and resorted to their native language whenever possible. Schools, with their mostly female teachers, were the main instrument of integration for the younger generation. This resulted in women often having greater respect than men; fathers often did not serve as role models, and their children's values tended to be influenced more by their peer groups.

The patriotic reverence of Americans for their Constitution binds together widely differing societal groups. This is apparent in such rituals as reciting the Pledge of Allegiance and displaying or waving the Stars and Stripes at every occasion. This is not, however, synonymous with nationalism in the sense of blind obedience to the state. For immigrants and their descendants, the flag was and is the symbol of their blending into a new nation, and the accompanying rituals express their American identity. These gestures are indicative of a new beginning, one that may go back as far as the landing of the Mayflower.

American society can be seen as a drama of new beginnings, a departure for new shores, a crossing of borders into a limitless future, and boundless, unbroken optimism—a story that Hollywood never tires of telling. This view of life has been called the "American Dream" and is fundamentally different from the typical German careerism and bureaucratic mentality. It might help to explain Americans' great mobility: their readiness to pull up stakes and leave their job, their town, and their church. People have the feeling that they are in charge of their own destiny, that no one will help them if they don't help themselves. The result is that less is expected of the state, both at the local and national level. And this is the point that Germans are least likely to comprehend: for Americans the "state" as a power does not have the weight that it has in many European countries.

In Europe, individual states had existed for centuries and controlled the societies within them. In America, immigrant societies had to do their part in creating a state and passing laws to maintain the peace. This primal scene forms the plot of countless Westerns, as the sheriff, Colt '45 in hand, enforces the law. As every American knows, the sheriff is paid by the community. His general relationship to the state is one of skepticism—he would rather depend on himself. This may well be a partial explanation of why so many Americans feel they have the right to carry a weapon.

The existence of an interactive society increases the readiness of neighbors to get together to solve local problems by themselves, instead of relying on the German "night watchman" state. This originated in pioneer and frontier days and has given Americans an openness and willingness to help one another in a way that is rare in Germany. Two American neighbors who are just getting to know each other develop a level of trust and intimacy far more quickly than their German counterparts. The latter may view such rapid accommodation as evidence of shallowness and superficiality. But in fact the Germans and Americans in question are using different cultural codes. The American code is appropriate to a mobile society that taps into the notion of solidarity early in an acquaintance. One could argue that

Americans are more social, since their friendliness is not tied to an exclusive friendship; they consider it, rather, a general virtue that is not linked to a particular person. Germans are always surprised that when Americans are away they will leave the keys to their house or apartment with a neighbor they have known for only a short time. Social interaction in America is uncomplicated and characterized by a readiness to expect the best from the other person—an attitude that tends to be less common in Germany. Americans quickly reach a level of familiarity and shift from using last names (Mr. Witherspoon) to first names (Herbert). Their sense of growing intimacy then often reduces the name to a single syllable (Herb).

The two cultures also differ in their response to success. For Germans, a successful person can be an object of envy and resentment, leading to doubts that everything was done on the up-and-up. But for Americans, the success of others is an inspiration to do the same. They love successful people because they give everyone else hope. This makes Americans fundamentally optimistic, and optimism is a sign of confidence in one's own abilities. They do not understand the German tendency toward melancholy, grouchiness, gloom, and whining. If there is a problem, people tackle it in a practical way rather than complaining about it. This applies as well to one's own psychological problems, since they are considered curable. America is an Eldorado for psychiatrists and psychologists who offer hope that one can start a new life at any time.

To a degree far greater than in Germany, a large segment of American society consists of active, practicing Christians. American religiosity expresses itself in a variety of different denominations of widely differing character. There are Baptists, Methodists, Quakers, Mormons, Lutherans, Presbyterians, Seventh-Day Adventists, born-again Christians, Holy Rollers, Shakers, Amish, and many others. In addition to their religious function, congregations are also centers of social life and focal points for charitable giving to a variety of worthy causes. Religious faith is not at all incompatible with business acumen, and economic success can be seen as a sign of divine grace. All this grows out of a culture of personal conviction and an emphasis on inner experience that anchors religiosity firmly in modern society.

Another American institution that fosters a sense of community, especially among men, is the world of sports. This is where one finds an opening to the American psyche. The three great mass-spectator sports are baseball, basketball, and American football, which is a kind of war disguised as a game. Soccer was unknown for a long time, though it is currently making progress, especially among women athletes. Football and basketball in particular play an important role in the social lives of schools and colleges; rivalries between teams and even between cities are strong, but rarely turn vicious. This may well be yet another indication of American sensibility: showing respect for an opponent's abilities, and in the end doing all one can to get along.

Text inspired by Dietrich Schwanitz, *Bildung. Alles was man wissen muß.* Eichborn, Frankfurt am Main 1999.

The Legacy of 1848

Transplanted Ideas & Values in America's Past and Present

In March 1970, at a meeting with then Federal President of West Germany, Gustav Heinemann, in the Civic Room of Flensburg's City Hall, Dr. Heinemann said: „Only by adopting the long-since neglected, suppressed, and ignored democratic legacy of 1848 can German historical research open up new vistas pointing to the future and venture into unexplored territories of scholarship worthy of discovery."

Carl Schurz

The "Forty-Eighters" were a relatively small number of individuals who emigrated from Europe in the late 1840s and early 1850s after fighting unsuccessfully with both pen and sword for liberty, democracy, and national unity. Many of the German Forty-Eighters immigrated to the United States; a large number from the present-day state of Schleswig-Holstein chose Scott County, Iowa as their adopted home on the Mississippi (west of Chicago). After settling in America, these unique and talented individuals provided an intellectual transfusion affecting not only their fellow German immigrants, but also the political and social history of the United States during one of its most critical periods.

Many of the Forty-Eighters left lasting marks in the fields of politics, education, business, journalism, the arts, and the military. Carl Schurz, perhaps the best-known of the German Forty-Eighters who settled in America, achieved great success in no less than four of these areas. During his long and illustrious career, he was a young ambassador to Spain for President Lincoln, a general during the Civil War, a United States senator, and Secretary of the Interior under President Rutherford B. Hayes. During his long and illustrious journalistic career, he served as chief editor of the *Detroit Post*, editor and co-proprietor of the *Westliche Post* in St. Louis, editor-in-chief and one of the proprietors of the *New York Evening Post*, and as an editorial writer for *Harper's Weekly*. Noted for his high principles, moral conscience, and avoidance of political partisanship, Schurz, like many of his fellow Forty-Eighters, can still teach us much with regard to dealing with the problems that confront us all today. His wife, too, was influential, in that she helped found the American kindergarten system.

The significance of the legacy of the 1848er Carl Schurz has become more timely. With the steady increase of immigration to the United States and the ongoing refugee crisis in Germany, it has become ever more important to establish the proper framework for the absorption and integration of newcomers. Schurz's solution — assimilation with the retention of the newcomers' ethnic heritage — is as valid today as it was when he articulated it in the nineteenth century. The fusion of ethnic identities and American / German values is of the greatest importance, and Carl Schurz's life is a worthy paradigm for all immigrants to emulate.

Carl Schurz Monument in Berlin?

In the spring of 2016, an influential German weekly news source published a valuable article about the legacy of 1848 and the German Forty-Eighters in America:

DER SPIEGEL (Dirk Kurbjuweit) inspired the German Federal President, Dr. Frank-Walter Steinmeier, to support the creation of a Forty-Eighter Monument. The article suggests the monument be placed in Berlin.

Hecker

Sigel

Struve

Schurz

ERINNERUNG
Steinmeier und die Forty-Eighters

Bundesaußenminister Frank-Walter Steinmeier unterstützt die Idee, den sogenannten Forty-Eighters ein Denkmal zu errichten. Es geht dabei um frühe deutsche Demokraten wie Carl Schurz, Friedrich Hecker, Gustav Struve und Franz Sigel, die an der gescheiterten Revolution von 1848/49 beteiligt waren. Sie emigrierten danach in die USA und kämpften im Bürgerkrieg gegen die Sklavenhalterei. Steinmeier: „Im historischen Gedächtnis vieler Menschen haben die Amerikaner, unterstützt von den Briten und Franzosen, 1945 die Demokratie nach Deutschland gebracht. Dabei gab es aber schon vor 1933 eine parlamentarische Erfahrungsbasis, die von den Akteuren 1848 hart erkämpft wurde. Deshalb ist das Denkmal für die sogenannten Forty-Eighters eine große Chance, an die wechselseitige Einflussnahme beim Aufbau stabiler Demokratien auf beiden Seiten des Ozeans zu erinnern." Den Vorschlag für ein solches Denkmal in der Hauptstadt hatte der SPIEGEL in der AUSGABE 14/2016 gemacht. Unter den Unterstützern, die sich daraufhin meldeten, sind der Schauspieler Ulrich Matthes und Erardo Cristoforo Rautenberg, der Generalstaatsanwalt von Brandenburg. Rautenberg hat bereits ein Konzept für eine Erinnerungsstätte entwickelt. In den USA gibt es mehrere Denkmäler für Carl Schurz, der es dort bis zum Senator und Innenminister gebracht hat. Rautenberg schlägt vor, eine dieser amerikanischen Büsten zu kopieren und in Berlin auf einen Sockel zu stellen. Eine Tafel solle an andere bekannte Forty-Eighters erinnern. ♦

Der Spiegel, April 23rd, 2016.
Detailed information: www.moin-moin.us

Wolfgang Börnsen (second from left), long-time member of the German Parliament, March 18, 2012, in Berlin, on the "Platz des 18. März" (behind the Brandenburg Gate). Börnsen suggested March 18th as a federal day of remembrance. (In memory of the "Barrikadenkämpfe", on March 18th and 19th, 1848, students, citizens, and laborers joined together in Berlin to defeat the Prussian army in the democratic revolution of 1848.) Volker Schroeder's www.maerzrevolution.de

Northfield News

PEOPLE

Wednesday, December 22, 1999

Kissinger on Carleton College: 'das ist gut'

FROM STAFF REPORTS

NORTHFIELD — In 1952 two young historians from two separate countries met at Harvard University. Gerhard Stoltenberg from Kiel University, in the Schleswig-Holstein region of Germany, and Henry Kissinger. Both men went on to have extremely successful political careers in their respective countries.

Behind the backdrop of these 47 years of close friendship, former Carleton professor Yogi Reppmann, and his former student of German, Matt Sarno, had been invited to the office of former Secretary of State Kissinger on New York's Park Ave. They produced a five minute video in which Kissinger, speaking his native German, expressed his deep admiration for his German colleague and friend Stoltenberg. The video was presented as a surprise on Dec. 12 in Flensburg, Germany before 1500 guests in honor of Stoltenberg's latest publication.

Stoltenberg, who is a likely candidate for the Chancellor of Germany himself, has written a book about his political career in which he explains the value of his early visit to the U.S. in 1952 and his friendship with Henry Kissinger.

What began as Reppmann and Sarno's five minute video-taping with Kissinger turned into a ninety minute conversation that ranged from the recent financial scandal involving former German Chancellor Helmut Kohl to the Baltic Sea Cooperation. Kissinger was amazed to hear that trade around the Baltic Sea region [is] larger than Germany's trade with Japan and the U.S. together. The topic had been taught in Reppmann's class about the European Union at Carleton College.

Kissinger, who not only concluded the meeting with the Northfield and Carleton College as well "Carleton in Minnesota? Das ist gut! (That is good!)"

From left to right: Matt Sarno, New York; Dr. Henry Kissinger, and Yogi Reppmann in the office of Kissinger Associates, Park Ave. (Submitted photo)

"1999, Yogi and a student of his pose for a picture with former U.S. Secretary of State Dr. Henry Kissinger in his New York office.

Yogi was first introduced to Dr. Kissinger by Gerhard Stoltenberg, a fatherly friend to both Yogi ad Dee Eicke. Stoltenberg, who served as Minister-President of Schleswig-Holstein, first met Kissinger when he was teaching at Harvard in 1953, and the two historians established a close friendship. In December of 1999, Yogi was present at a book party given by his newspaper editor friend, Stephan Richter, who had just published what proved to be Stoltenberg's last book. During this party, a video shot by Yogi with Kissinger's greetings from New York caused tears to well up in the eyes of the old politician. - Yogi loves to tell his Kissinger marzipan story. At the end of his meeting with the great man in 1999, Yogi presented him with a gift of Lübeck's finest marzipan. Kissinger, who had been little standoffish prior to that moment, left the room, returned visibly moved, and asked 'How did you know?' Unbeknownst to Yogi, Lübeck marzipan was a very fond childhood memory for Henry Kissinger. He related how only once a year — at the time before Christmas — could his parents in Germany afford to buy the world's best marzipan, Lübeck marzipan. - Every time Yogi returns to New York, he always stops by Kissinger's office and brings him some marzipan, or if not in the country, mails him some before Christmas. Unfailingly, Kissinger responds with a sweet letter." In: Scott C. Christiansen, *Soul of Schleswig-Holstein*, p. 148. (fascinating coffee table book: Printing on Demand, www.Lulu.com).

"Dear Yogi, Congratulations on the re-dedication of the monument to the Schleswig-Holsteiners who came to Davenport in 1848-1850 to escape the oppressive conditions in their homeland. Their descendants and others of German stock who arrived in America in the mid-19th century have been one of America's most successful immigrant groups. They deserve this monument, ... Thank you for the marzipan. I have no better source for the real thing, but can always count on you! ... I hope you will have a most enjoyable summer in Flensburg., Warm Regards, [signed] Henry Kissinger" (letter from April 30, 2008) ... I read the booklet that you co-wrote with Friedhelm Caspari, *The Holocaust Boxcar: A Powerful Admonition Against Anti-Semitism*, with interest, and look forward to the updates you send on the German-American Forty-Eighters. Congratulations on all of the good work you do. [signed] Sincerely, Henry. A. Kissinger" (letter from November 3, 2016)

Publications About 1848ers

- Don Heinrich Tolzmann, *The German-American Forty-Eighters, 150th Anniversary*, in: German-Americana: Selected Essays. (Milford, Ohio: Little Miami Pub. Co., 2009), p. 25-28. Also: *The German-American Forty-Eighters: 1848-1998.* (Indianapolis, 1997). www.DonHeinrichTolzmann.net

- *Theodor Olshausen, 1802-1869 – Briefe an den Bruder Justus*, Ingo Reppmann, Joachim Reppmann, Hg., Flensburg, 2003, p. 181 - 201. (1989, a piece of good fortune: while visiting friends in Leipzig a few weeks before the peaceful revolution was to begin, Bernd Philipsen, Flensburg, and I went to the former Zentrales Staatsarchiv, Dienststelle Merseburg, where we discovered Theodore Olshausen's letters to his brother Justus, 1821-1869.)

- *North Germans in America, Freedom, Education, and Well-being for All! - Forty-Eighters from Schleswig-Holstein in the USA, 1847-1860,* Joachim Reppmann, Davenport, IA, 1999. (Freiheit, Bildung und Wohlstand für Alle! Schleswig-Holsteinische 1848er in den USA, 1847-1860, Joachim Reppmann, Flensburg, 1994.)

- *Hans Reimer Claussen, 1804-1894, Eine Lebensskizze, A Sketch of His Life,* Joachim Reppmann, La Vem Rippley, Hg., Flensburg, 1994 (in German and English.)

- *1848 – 1998: the 150th Anniversary of the Revolution, Friedrich Hedde – Schleswig-Holsteiner in Amerika,* Joachim Reppmann and Heinz–Werner Arens, Hg., Flensburg, 1998 (in German and English.)

- Stuart Gorman and Joachim Reppmann, *Triumph of Will – Printer's boy to publisher: The remarkable story of German immigrant Henry Finnern* (Davenport, IA: Hesperian Press, 2009).

- *Turnvater Müller am Mississippi–the Legacy of 1848, Through Today*, 22 pages – Essay with informative colored maps, etc. in English, Danish, and German, Klaus Lemke-Paetznick & Joachim Reppmann, Flensburg 2013.

- *Der Wilde Westen beginnt in Flensburg - Über Amerikas Seele und die deutsch-amerikanische Freundschaft*, Joachim Reppmann, 48 S., Flensburg, 2013.

- *Stoltenberg Yearbook 2016*, The Stoltenberg Institute for German-American Forty-Eighter Studies, Northfield, MN and Flensburg, SH, 2016. (Printing on Demand: www.LuLu.com)

- Joachim Reppmann, John D. Barbour, Hg., *Toiling with the Defeated/ Schuften mit den Besiegten, US-Tagebücher von Deane und Ian Barbour aus den Ruinen von Hamburg und Münster, 1948*, Northfield, MN und Flensburg, SH, 2016. (Printing on Demand: www.LuLu.com)

- Joachim Reppmann, *Eric Braeden, From Bredenbek to Hollywood: The Legacy of 1848, Through Today*, Northfield, MN and Flensburg, SH, 2016. (Printing on Demand: www.LuLu.com)

- Friedhelm Caspari and Joachim Reppmann, *The Holocaust Boxcar: A Powerful Admonition Against Anti-Semitism, Northfield, MN, 2017* . (Printing on Demand: www.LuLu.com)

- Scott C. Christiansen, *The Soul of Schleswig-Holstein: An Iowan's Insight into His Ancestral Homeland*, Up Ewig Ungedeelt Press, Iowa City, Iowa, 2009. (Printing on Demand: www.LuLu.com)

> *In this fascinating history, Christiansen explores not only his immigrant ancestor, but also the Forty-Eighters and their importance for Germany and America, placing his work in the context of an in-depth portrait of Schleswig-Holstein. Richly illustrated with almost eight hundred colored photographs and maps and with a detailed index (p. 239-283), this coffee table book clearly demonstrates the significance of the Forty-Eighters, as well as the importance of Schleswig-Holstein for the history of the German immigration to America, especially for the state of Iowa. A beautifully written work, Christiansen also presents a perceptive exploration of the values of the German Forty-Eighters and their relevance for today. Available from: www.LuLu.com (Printing on Demand).*
>
> *Don Heinrich Tolzmann, Book Review Editor, in: German Life, November/December 2009.*

Appendix 3

German-American Friendship Projects

- 1983: Organization of excursion to Germany for forty-five Low German "Schleswig-Holsteiners" from Iowa.

- 1990: Community Colleges, Iowa, three-week visit. The topic was *The Fall of the Berlin Wall* (forty-one lectures and slide shows).

- 1991: First family reunion of the American/Schleswig-Holstein Meggers family in Iowa and Wisconsin: 430 Meggers from sixteen U.S. states and Germany.

- 1992: Four-week U.S. lecture tour (fifty-two lectures and slide shows) organized by community colleges with a topic of *Germany in Europe*.

- 1994: Claussen Centennial: 1848er Conference in Davenport, IA.

- 1997: Fifty-four students as the first U.S. football team to Northern Germany and Denmark.

- 2001: Organized a Low German Conference in Grand Island, NE.

- 2003: Founded de.us inc., INTERNATIONAL CONNECTIONS with Steven Bosacker, Chief of Staff, Gov. Ventura; an organization that finds, facilitates, and incubates new business connections between the Baltic Sea Region and America's Midwest.

- 2005: Donation drive for New Orleans with German newspaper chain: $160,000. (See brief Stephan Richter & Jim Amoss commentary, p. 65)

- 2006: Thank You Gala with four thousand readers and editor Jim Amoss (Times-Picayune, New Orleans) in Flensburg, Germany.

- 2008: U.S. visit of twenty-one German health care CEOs.

- 2009: The Legacy of 1848 - Henry Finnern Conference (Denison, IA).

- 2010: Opening of German-American Heritage Museum, Washington, DC, Board Member.

- 2013: *Forty-Eighters and Friends*, 30 minute video paid by Deutsche Welle TV (Erich Bettermann) - a conference at Wartburg College, Waverly, IA: "The international Legacy of 1848 Through Today". (Videos - www. Moin-Moin.us)

- Organization of the international Legacy of 1848 Through Today Conference (Wartburg College, Waverly, IA)

- Founder of the Stoltenberg Institute for German-American Forty-Eighter Studies.

- 2014: The Steuben Society of America presented its Erick Kurz Memorial Award for German-American History in New York for the research on the 1848 movement's democratic impact in Germany and the USA.

- 2015: Organized the transportation of a "Holocaust Boxcar" from Thuringia to *Fagen Fighters WWII Museum*, Granite Falls, MN.

- 2016: Low German monument in Cole Camp, MO (keynote address).

- 2017: German-American Conference in Northfield, MN: Holocaust Education & The Legacy of 1848, Through Today; *German-American Friendship Award of the Federal Republic.*

Appendix 4

Highlights: 2017 Conference

Holocaust Education &

The Legacy of 1848, Through Today

After three days of stimulating and thought-provoking presentations, displays, and discussions, the "Legacy of 1848" conference concluded in Northfield, Minnesota, on April 2, 2017.

Conference speakers from left: Dee Eicke, Germany; Eric Braeden, Hollywood; Yogi Reppmann, Northfield, MN; and Herbert Quelle, Chicago, Consul General.

Sponsored by the Stoltenberg Institute for German-American For-ty-eighter Studies and organized by Drs. Joachim "Yogi" Reppmann (North-field, Minnesota) and Don Heinrich Tolzmann (Cincinnati, Ohio), the confer-ence attracted speakers, participants, and guests from the United States, Germany, and Denmark.

Always educational and often highly emotional, the conference stimu-lated everyone to reflect on the challenges that confronted our forebears, how they dealt with and often overcame them, and how mankind can learn and profit from the collective legacy of these brave men and women. As was made obvious to all conference attendees, our ancestors' challenges didn't exist in a vacuum of time, only to disappear at their deaths. Acknowledging these trials, studying their root causes, and familiarizing ourselves with the methods used in combating them, are indispensable for a world where cul-tural differences are celebrated, not vilified.

Throughout the conference, echoes of the philosopher George Santaya-na's statement that "those who do not learn history are doomed to repeat it" reverberated throughout Northfield's St. John's Lutheran Church. This famous admonition, which has been thoughtlessly repeated to the point of becoming a mind-numbing bromide, took on new currency throughout "The Legacy of 1848 through Today." As the conference organizers intended, the word "legacy" assumed great importance, for the real and lasting legacy of the influential immigrants of 1848 was their elevation of freedom as the most unifying and integral component in a world community comprised of so many diverse parts.

* * * * *

The conference opened at four o'clock on March 30, 2017, in the con-ference center of Northfield's lovely St. John's Lutheran Church. After an hour-long welcome reception, where presenters, participants, and attend-ees re-established old connections and forged new ones, Pastor Klaus Lemke-Paetznick (Wilhelmshaven, Germany) gave an insightful talk about Martin Luther's childhood. This timely presentation — Luther posted his ninety-five theses five hundred years ago on October 31, 1517 — was en-hanced by a pictorial exhibit, which chronologically highlighted significant moments in his childhood of the seminal Protestant reformer.

The conference kicked off in earnest at 8:30 on the following morning. Deftly moderated by Dee Eicke, Pastor Lemke-Paetznick, and Dr. Reppmann, the ensuing presentations and discussions of the first day were primarily devoted to Holocaust education. Participants and presenters included Steve Hunegs (executive director, Jewish Community Relations Council for Minnesota and the Dakotas, Minneapolis), Herbert Quelle (German Consul General, Chicago), Carol Kahn-Strauss (Leo Baeck Institute, New York City), Charles Fodor (Hungarian Holocaust survivor), Dr. Gabrielle Robinson (Jewish Federation, South Bend, Indiana), Dr. R. Don Keysser (GACC, Bloomington, Minnesota), Prof. Dr. Gerd-Winand Imeyer (Honorary Consul General of Bulgaria, Hamburg Chamber of Commerce), and Dr. Esther Seha (Minneapolis).

The presentations and discussions were peppered with personal and familial stories, which placed the stain of the Holocaust in a most moving context. Particularly poignant was the presentation of Charles Fodor, whose presence at the conference would not have been possible were it not for the chance intercession of a compassionate but nameless individual more than seventy years earlier. Dr. Peter Lubrecht's talk about growing up as a German-American in New York City drove home the point that the repercussions of the Holocaust often migrated across the Atlantic affecting many German-Americans in an insidious, if less visceral way.

After a top-notch keynote address delivered by Chicago's Consul General Herbert Quelle, the evening concluded with the world premiere of Stephan Witthoeft's documentary, *A Flensburg Perspective: Erna de Vries and the Holocaust Boxcar*. This moving film not only highlighted the Holocaust's horrors, but also documented the efforts to bring a Holocaust boxcar (used to transport German Jews to concentration camps) to the *Fagen Fighters World War II Museum* in Granite Falls, Minnesota. Playing a significant role in the acquisition of this important historical artifact was one of the conference's organizers, Dr. Joachim "Yogi" Reppmann. A one hundred and two-page pamphlet chronicling the background of the Holocaust boxcar was also presented to the conference's attendees. The boxcar exhibit at the Fagen's museum will be an important and tangible historical reminder that "anyone who does not remember that inhumanity exists, is susceptible to being infected again."

The day concluded with the sixtieth birthday party for conference co-organizer Dr. Reppmann, which was held at Northfield's Froggy Bottoms River Pub. Providing entertainment for the celebration was local guitarist/singer Todd Thomson, who was accompanied by Herbert Quelle on the harmonica. Quelle, a leading German diplomat, recently authored Monika's Blues, a book seamlessly weaving the harmonica's importance in the history of blues music with the author's reflections on African-Americans' struggle for freedom.

* * * * *

The second full day of the conference was devoted to the legacy and significance of America's most consequential immigrants, the Forty-eight-ers. Enlightening and thought-provoking presentations were given by Dr. Peter Lubrecht (Newton, New Jersey), Prof. Dr. Wolfgang Müller-Michaelis (Hamburg), Felix Zimmermann (Freiburg), Pastor Klaus Lemke-Paetznick (Wilhelmshaven), Jan Jessen (Denmark), Larry Grill (Schleswig, Iowa), conference co-organizer Dr. Don Heinrich Tolzmann (Cincinnati), Dr. Gabrielle Robinson (South Bend, Indiana), Wade Olsen, Denny Warta and George Glotzbach (New Ulm, Minnesota), Terry Sveine (New Ulm), Dietrich Eicke (Lübeck), Dr. Julie Klassen (Northfield, Minnesota), and Marcus Bracklo (Bad Soden). The presentations and discussions were as interesting as they were varied, with everyone gaining a greater appreciation for the contributions made by the Forty-eighters and the great legacy they bequeathed to subsequent generations.

After a wonderful dinner and genuine fellowship among the conference participants and attendees, Carol Kahn-Strauss (who'd previously received Germany's highest civilian award, the Commander's Cross of the Order of Merit) and Diane Fagen (president of the *Fagen Fighters WWII Museum* in Granite Falls, Minnesota) were presented with the Carl Schurz Award. Both women made heartfelt speeches confirming the soundness of their choice as recipients of the award named in honor of America's most significant and well-known Forty-eighter, Carl Schurz.

Following this presentation, German Consul General, Herbert Quelle (Chicago) presented conference co-organizer Dr. Joachim "Yogi" Reppmann with the German-American Friendship Award of the Federal Republic of Germany for his contributions to German-American relations. As Yogi's friend, I was particularly glad to see him honored in this way. It's long been my view that his outsized personality has often obscured the many real and tangible contributions he's made not only in the historical field, but also in the establishment of bridges furthering contact between and understanding of peoples on both sides of the Atlantic.

* * * * *

The conference concluded with "Thoughts on Being German," a poignant and heartfelt address delivered by Hans Jörg Gudegast, aka Eric Braeden. Born in Bredenbek, Schleswig-Holstein, Gudegast experienced firsthand the horrors of World War II prior to his immigration to the United States in 1959. Energetic, athletic, intellectually inquisitive, and analytical, he fought stereotypes and incredibly long odds to become one of Hollywood's most beloved and well-known stars. He has appeared in scores of movies and TV shows, including thirty-seven years in the signature role of "Victor Newman" on The Young and the Restless.

Braeden's experiences and deep understanding provided a fitting denouement for a conference whose first day emphasized the Holocaust. Throughout his adult life, the humanitarian and activist has worked hard in promoting a positive, realistic, and balanced image of German-Americans and advancing German-Jewish dialogue. A man of strong convictions, Braeden believes "Nazi Germany would not have existed had we had a democracy. Had Germany remained a democracy, we wouldn't be talking about the Holocaust. We wouldn't be talking about any of this."

Braeden's life experiences also dovetailed beautifully with the focus of the conference's second day, the important and influential immigrant group known as the Forty-eighters. Like the Forty-eighters who were honored at the conference — immigrants who were shocked slavery could exist in a country ostensibly embracing the ideas embodied in the Constitution and Declaration of Independence — Braeden, too, faced similar disillusioning moments. "I came here in 1959. I took the Greyhound bus from New York to Galveston, Texas, to the South, and I thought I had landed in a full democracy, and here I see signs for 'Whites Only,' for 'Coloreds only,' and the separation was stark."

Having spent the better part of the last two decades trying to understand the Forty-eighters, it's my belief Braeden could well have been a member of this significant immigrant group had he been born 120 years earlier. Like so many of the Forty-eighters I've studied, Braeden is straightforward, direct — some might even say blunt — yet at the same time, richly nuanced in so many ways. Having lived in America for over half a century, his fervent love for his adopted country has never blinded him to the fact that the struggle to live up to the ideals embodied in our founding documents is a never-ending one requiring constant vigilance. Like so many of the Forty-eighters, Braeden has never been content to sit on the sidelines.

He takes a very active interest in politics and helps rally support for those he feels will best serve the needs of his adopted country.

As a German-American who embraces the best of both cultures, Braeden has devoted much of his time to strengthening the ties between the German and American peoples, and his exemplary efforts in this regard have been honored on many occasions. He's been awarded the Federal Medal of Honor from Germany's President on two separate occasions, been invited to the White House by President Reagan to celebrate German-American Heritage Day, and received the Ellis Island Medal of Honor in 2007.

Yet, as much as Eric Braeden fosters German-American relations and as much as he is a loyal American citizen, he will also always be a German. Having a deep appreciation of, respect for, and loyalty to both countries is an inherent part of the man's complexity. The inherent duality of his life was evidenced time and time again throughout his concluding address, as reflected in the numerous times he had to pause and gather himself while conveying the essence of what it means to an American who will also always be a German.

As Braeden concluded his talk, I remembered a previous remark of his I'd run across while writing a brief biographical sketch of him some years ago: "I grew up tough. I'll fight you to the last — I'll never give up." What an apropos sentiment for a conference devoted to the study of the Forty-eighters and Holocaust survivors. It is precisely this trait — that of never giving up, of triumphing over long odds through the sheer force of one's will — that conference attendees and participants celebrated at "The Legacy of 1848 Through Today."   www.Moin-Moin.us

— Scott C. Christiansen, Iowa City, IA

On April 1, Consul General Herbert Quelle presented Dr. Joachim "Yogi" Reppmann with the German American Friendship Award. The Prize, established in 1981, is given by the German Ambassador to those who have shown extraordinary commitment to fostering German-American relations.

Appendix 5

Holocaust Boxcar
Headed for Minnesota

The period of National Socialism in Germany and the horrors of the Hitler regime cannot be understood apart from the political and societal developments that preceded them. The events that took place between the wars and during the Nazi dictatorship have been analyzed, illuminated, and described many times. Literature on the structure of the Nazi system and its leading figure, the "populist" Adolf Hitler, has been published extensively and in many languages. For the first time, however, Friedhelm Caspari & Joachim Reppmann are offering for American readers in particular a fact book, "The Holocaust Boxcar: A Powerful Admonition Against Anti-Semitism," that briefly explains the most important developments in Germany during the nineteenth and twentieth centuries.

In the fall of 2015, an abandoned German boxcar dating from the year 1899 had begun its long journey halfway around the world from the Thuringian Forest to the *Fagen Fighters World War II Museum* in Granite Falls, Minnesota. Joachim "Yogi" Reppmann had learned of the boxcar from his uncle Peter Prass from Gera, who had spent thirty-four years working on the railroad behind the Iron Curtain in East Germany.

Having teamed with Diane Fagen, president of the museum, Yogi arranged to have this horrific reminder of the Holocaust transported to the museum in Granite Falls. The boxcar had originally been used as a normal rail vehicle for merchandise, but eventually carried victims identified for elimination by the Nazis to the concentration camp at Auschwitz. On May

21, 2016, the *Fagen Fighters WWII Museum* opened its Holocaust Boxcar and POW exhibit, the most recent addition to its historical aviation displays. In its present location, the boxcar serves as a "lesson in history" and should be understood by the public as such. In the context of the Fagen Fighters exhibition, the present compendium would be highly appropriate as reading material in American high school and college programs, where it would offer an instructive commentary on some of the most cataclysmic events in German history. Today this topic is more relevant than ever, considering the lack of understanding, the hatred and intolerance among populist movements and agitators that has developed in connection with the recent waves of refugees worldwide.

As the war ended, Berlin lay in ruins and Hitler had committed suicide. In the first days of May 1945, the north German city of Flensburg wrote a chapter of its own history. This city on the border with Denmark received thousands of German refugees from the eastern territories and people who had been freed from concentration camps. At the same time, however, hundreds of top-brass Nazis went into hiding in the city, which became the new "capital of the Reich" for a few days. A television documentation of this unusual complex of events in Flensburg, was produced in March 2017 by Stephan Witthöft, SALVE MEDIA, Erfurt: *A Flensburg Perspective: Erna de Vries and the Holocaust Boxcar.* (www.Moin-Moin.us English Videos)

Georgenthal, State of Thuringia, from left to right: Ron and Diane Fagen, Minister-President Christine Lieberknecht, and Yogi Reppmann, September 24, 2015.

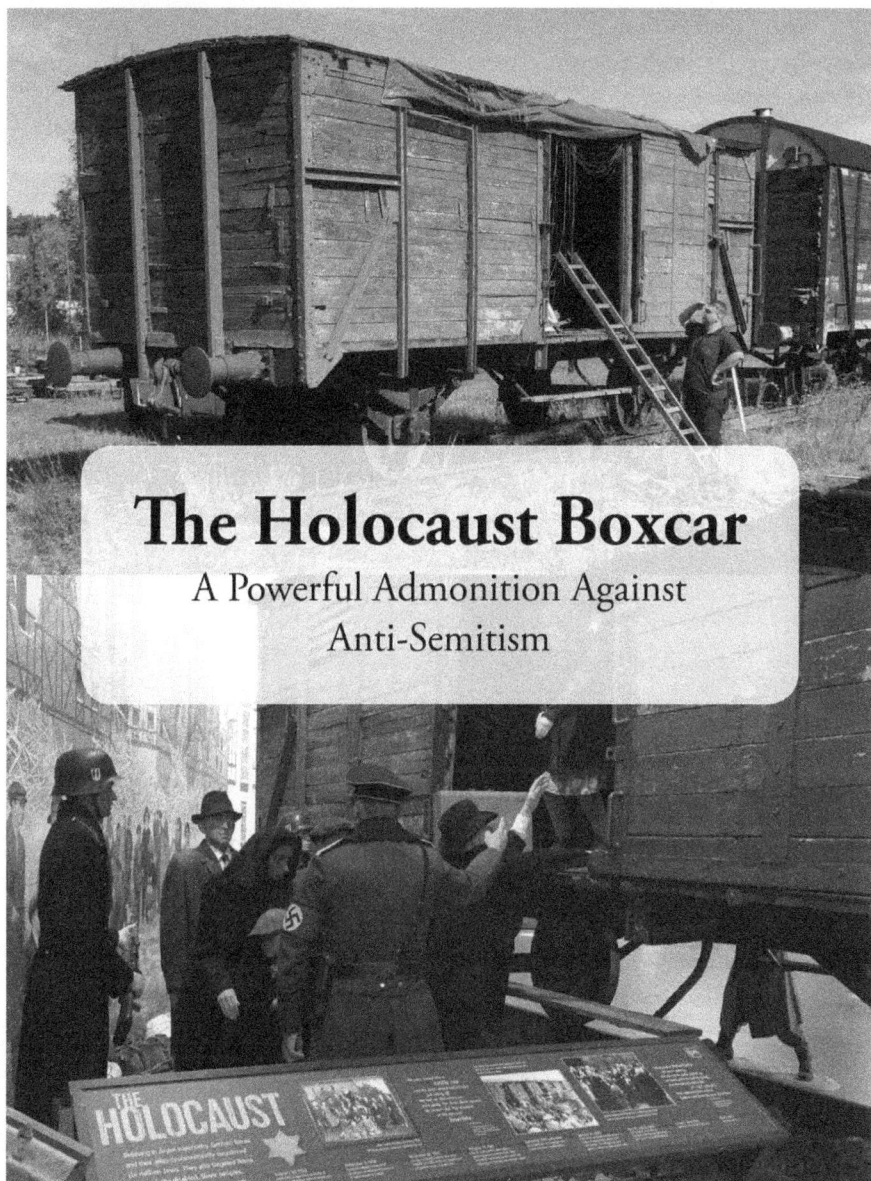

The Holocaust Boxcar
A Powerful Admonition Against Anti-Semitism

Top: The boxcar from 1899 near Georgenthal, Thuringia.
Bottom: Grand Opening of the Holocaust and POW Boxcar Exhibit, on May 21st, 2016, in the Fagen Fighters WWII Museum, Granite Falls, MN. - The New Fact Book about the Origins of the Nazi Regime and the Conclusion of its Murderous Dictatorship, "The Holocaust Boxcar: A Powerful Admonition Against Anti-Semitism", by Friedhelm Caspari & Joachim Reppmann, can be ordered via www.LuLu.com (Printing on Demand), $10,00.

Joachim (Yogi) Reppmann, Ph.D., was born in Flensburg, Schleswig-Holstein, in 1957. He attended Altes Gymnasium, a school founded by Danish King Frederick II in 1566. He matriculated at the University of Kiel, where he studied history and American literature. In 1984, he completed his masters thesis entitled *Transplanted Ideas: The Concept of Freedom and Democracy of the Schleswig-Holstein Forty-Eighters — Origins and Effects 1846-1856*. He has written several books on notable Schleswig-Holstein emigrants and the mass migration to the United States; served as a professor of German at St. Olaf and Carleton Colleges in Northfield, Minnesota; and chaired several conferences on topics ranging from the Low German language to Forty-Eighter Hans Reimer Claussen. Since 1983, Yogi has organized both individualized language study-abroad programs and educational exchanges between the United States and Germany for groups as diverse as farmers from Holstein, Iowa; American teachers of German; college football players; and representatives of the Mayo Clinic in Rochester, Minnesota. Since 2010, the founding of the amazing *German-American Heritage Museum, Washington, DC, www.gahmusa.org*, Yogi has served on its Board. Always looking to strengthen ties between the two areas he calls home — the Baltic Sea region in northern German and America's Midwest — Yogi co-founded *de.us, International Connections* to incubate new business connections between the two regions. 1995: marriage to Gitta in Las Vegas.   www.Moin-Moin.us

The text of the present booklet was translated by **Norman Watt,** Ph.D.. He was born in 1938 in New Jersey, taught German language and literature from 1966 to 2000 at St. Olaf College, Northflied, MN. Main literary interests: German poetry and German and Austrian literature of the late nineteenth and early twentieth centuries; has translated novellas by Arthur Schnitzler and has written a novel, as yet unpublished. May be contacted at: watt@stolaf.edu.

Danke

Ben Parsell

Petra Imeyer

Evelyn Sadri

Norman Watt

Peter Stoll

Klaus Lemke-Paetznick

Dietrich Eicke

Claus Peter Kölln

Alexandra Kortum

Hans-Jürgen Ahrens

Stephan Witthöft

Marion Schneider

Udo Petersen

German-American Heritage Museum

German-American Heritage Museum
719 6th St. NW,
Washington, D.C., 20001, USA
www.gahfusa.org
(202) 467-5000

Please consider a membership for yourself or your loved ones in the German-American Heritage Foundation of the USA, GAHF, which runs a first-rate museum in Washington, D.C. (The museum occupies a former villa owned by a German-American beer brewer and is not far away from the White House). Annual individual membership starts at $50 (Associate Member [non-voting]). Membership includes an informative newsletter on glossy paper, an invitation to a wonderful gala (German-American of the Year), along with exhibits and events, sometimes including a "Frühschoppen" (morning pint) on a weekend!

www.gahmusa.org/product/individual-membership

www.ingramcontent.com/pod-product-compliance
Lightning Source LLC
Chambersburg PA
CBHW032145040426
42449CB00005B/410